IAN ALLAN TRANSPORT
LIBRARY

CHARLES H. ROE

Includes Optare

IAN ALLAN TRANSPORT
LIBRARY

Charles
H. Roe

Includes Optare

GEOFF LUMB

Ian Allan
PUBLISHING

Contents

Front cover:
Darlington Corporation No 47 VHN 401 was displayed at the 1954 CM Show. No 47 was the first double-deck motorbus to be purchased by the corporation and the Roe body with safety staircase seated 31/25 while the Guy Arab IV chassis was powered by a Gardner 5LW engine.

Back cover top:
Another Roe body displayed at the 1954 CM Show was Hull Corporation No 102 RKH 102 the first of the 15 production 'Coronation' type trolleybus with front entrance, centre exit bodies seating 30/24 built on Sunbeam MF2B chassis by Guy Motors Ltd.

Back cover bottom:
Grimsby Corporation continued to purchase centre-entrance double-deck motorbuses and in July 1937 received a further six AEC Regents, Nos 58-63, JV 5931-6, which were despatched from Crossgates. Grimsby was one of the last operators still to specify petrol-engined chassis.

Half-title:
When orders for single vehicles were received it was often advantageous to add this to a larger batch to simplify production. Hence, three Leeds-type bodies with panoramic windows were built for Weardale Motor Services in January 1970 for a member of A1 Motor Services, J. E. Docherty, in May 1973, and finally one for Colin Pegg in June 1974. All were built on Leyland Atlantean chassis and, other than minor details such as destination blinds, were like the Leeds buses processed at the same time. The Weardale Motor Services example, GUP 6H, is seen in January 1970 on its test run before certification at Crossgates.

Title page:
The 1950 changes in PSV dimensions allowed the length of double-deck buses to be increased from 26ft to 27ft. East Yorkshire Motor Services Ltd took advantage of this change when Roe built 16 double-deck coaches with Beverley Bar-profiled roofs, platform doors and fully enclosed cabs. The coaches seating 50 were mounted on Leyland PD2/12 chassis. They were painted in primrose and light blue and were nicknamed 'Yellow Perils' when delivered between January and June 1952. Five of them pose for the photographer before entering Newcastle on the express service from Hull. By 1954 they had been painted dark blue and demoted to bus routes.

First published 1999

ISBN 0 7110 2626 2

Published by Ian Allan Publishing
an imprint of Ian Allan Publishing Ltd, Terminal House, Shepperton, Surrey TW17 8AS.
Printed by Ian Allan Printing Ltd, Riverdene Business Park, Hersham, Surrey KT12 4RG.

Code: 9902/B2

Acknowledgements

The primary source of material used for this book was Companies' House, where staff at the Leeds office obtained information on the now dormant Charles H. Roe Ltd company which is still owned by British Aerospace, while the Cardiff office was able to identify and trace the earlier records to the Public Records Office at Kew. The Leeds City Library, local archive section, was extremely helpful in producing material on the activities at Balm Road, during World War 1, and on the activities of Number One Shell-filling factory at Barnbow. The Patents Library in Leeds provided copies of relevant patents. The West Yorkshire County Archives at Wakefield allowed access to the deeds of the various properties, while its Sheepscar, Leeds office produced for inspection all the planning applications made by C. H. Roe at Balm Road Mills.

The tracing of the information on the Roe family history which helped to piece together the early background is the work of Christine Aldridge, while P. B. Smith and Chris Heaps helped to find background information on early directors. Both Geoff Burrows and Chris Taylor contributed a number of interesting facts relevant to the early days.

Roy Marshall and John Senior both willingly made available material gathered for the 1979 book, published by The Transport Publishing Co.

The National Railway Museum library and photographic records were also extremely helpful in finding photographs of the Derwent Valley Light Railway railcars.

Gordon Baron at the British Commercial Vehicle Museum, Leyland deserves a special mention. As does M. Bray, industrial photographer, who provided superb prints from negatives or photographs which were over 60 years old.

The artwork for the various transfers and Roe company logos have been recreated by Tony Greaves who has also contributed the chapter on Optare Ltd and provided many photographs. His contribution has enhanced this book.

Where photographs are captioned without copyright credits they are invariably ones taken for or by the Roe company to promote its products. We are still extremely grateful for the help given by the company when the replica body was being designed using known data and photographs as the base, some 15 years ago.

Once again I am indebted to my daughters Clare and Jane and to my wife Ethel for all helping to translate my script and put it on to disc, and to the publisher, Ian Allan Publishing Ltd, for its help in producing this book.

Picture Credits:
All uncredited pictures are from the author's collection.

Below:
Leeds City Tramways & Transport Department placed its first orders for Roe bodywork in December 1926 when it specified 30-seat front-entrance bodies for the 12 Karrier JKL normal-control chassis it had ordered earlier. Delivery of these 12 vehicles began in February and was completed in April 1927. Numbered 41-52, they were used for one-man operation until the 1930 Road Traffic Act limited this to vehicles with 20 seats or less.

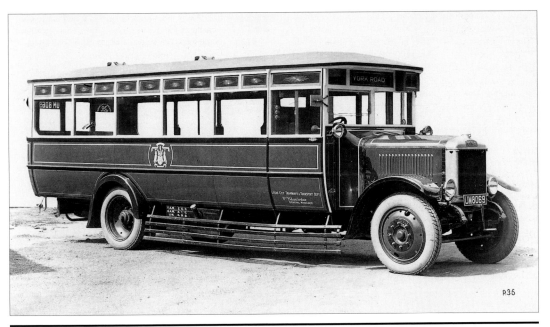

Introduction

CROSS GATES CARRIAGE WORKS

This book, the result of interests going back to 1946, is an attempt to produce a useful work of reference for future generations about the various activities of the Leeds coachbuilder, Charles H. Roe.

After the end of World War 2, a steady stream of new motorbus chassis from Leyland Motors Ltd was driven eastbound past my home on the A643 near Huddersfield. The drivers, wearing leather helmets, airforce flying suits, goggles and gloves, were sat on a crude wooden seat often just lashed to the chassis frame. A steady stream of new buses for Oldham Corporation and Lancashire United would then be seen heading west with large paper posters displayed in the windows advertising that the body had been built by Charles H. Roe Ltd, Crossgates, Leeds. Over the next few years it seemed that all the better quality new buses seen locally had bodywork built by Roe.

During the Easter 1952 school holidays, I made a telephone call to Crossgates Carriage Works requesting a works visit for myself and a friend, which was granted for 2pm the next day. Arriving at reception we were greeted by the Sales Manager, who had thought we were from Huddersfield Corporation rather than lived in Huddersfield! He quickly organised one of his staff to show us around the works. This visit and many subsequent visits were all made memorable by the courtesy and willingness of the staff to discuss the various stages in building bodies for motor and trolley-buses. Everyone working there was proud of the company's standing in the industry.

In early 1983, Ribble Motor Services Ltd asked the Roe works for copies of the body drawings used for the two original Leyland Lion PLSC3 buses bodied in May 1929 for York Corporation. Roe was unable to help,

and passed the request back to British Leyland who suggested that the author may be able to design a replica bus body for the Leyland PLSC3 chassis which Ribble had rebuilt and intended at that point to restore as York Corporation No 2 for hire to another NBC company in the Northern Region. Using contemporary published information, photographs, etc, detailed drawings were produced for Ribble Engineering to manufacture and assemble the replica body at its Frenchwood works in Preston. The finished product was accepted by the public as an original rebuild, although it was painted in Ribble livery when completed in early 1985.

Unfortunately this was a few months after British Leyland had closed the Crossgates Carriage Works in September 1984, and transferred its remaining body production orders to Workington. However, the vehicle is a reminder of the skills of Messrs Walker and Houghton who built the original York No 2 in 1929, and the many hundreds of skilled bodybuilders and craftsmen who worked in Leeds during the 68 years that Charles H. Roe Ltd was in business, producing quality products that sold themselves.

This reputation was put to good use when the former Roe Plant Director, Russell Richardson, was able to persuade the West Yorkshire Enterprise Board of the viability of a rescue package involving the former works and initially some of the redundant craftsmen who were all prepared to invest their savings and redundancy money in establishing a new company to give customers a choice, appropriately being called 'Optare' from the Latin 'to choose'.

Geoff Lumb
Huddersfield
June 1998

Above:
Line drawing of Roe works.

Right:
By March 1929, when Alf Harrison placed this Thornycroft model A6 touring coach into service with a 24-seat dual-door Roe body, the traditional charabanc had developed into this type of all-weather coach. UA 6750 was operated from Harrison's premises in Kirkstall Road, Leeds.

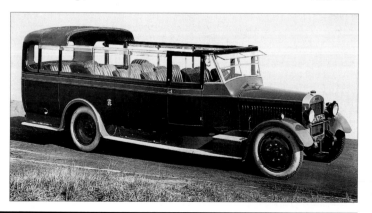

1. Early Background

Charles Henry Roe was born in York on 22 May 1887. His father, Charles Roe, was a railway carriage fitter at the North Eastern Railway Company's York carriage works a short walk from the family residence at 19 Nunthorpe Road, which was also conveniently close to Bishopgate and the city centre. His father was born at Sudborough, Northamptonshire, and his mother, Elizabeth née Blacker, was from York. The 1891 census recorded, when Charles Henry was three, that the family included three older children: Fanny Blacker aged eight, John Thomas aged six, Mary E. aged four, and one younger, Eveline A. aged one. His father and mother were 32 and 31.

By 1909, Charles Henry's father had been made a foreman at the carriage works, and the family had moved to 6 East Mount Road.

Charles Henry gained a grounding in railway rolling stock at York and in 1912 moved to Charles Roberts and Co Ltd at Horbury Junction near Wakefield where he was employed as a draughtsman. Charles Roberts was one of the private companies building and supplying railway rolling stock to many of the railway companies at home and abroad.

In late 1913, Charles Henry Roe changed jobs again, this time moving to the Leeds works of the RET Construction Co Ltd where he became one of the two engineering assistants to the company's Chief Engineer, Mr Edward May Munro MIMechE, MIEE. Charles H. Roe found that his new job involved spending time at the company's London office as well as in Bristol where Mr Munro was the Managing Director of Brecknell, Munro & Rogers Ltd.

By the end of 1913, 27 trolleybuses had been supplied to eight customers by RET Construction Co Ltd and its predecessor, Railless Electric Traction.

Charles H. Roe was closely involved in the redesign of the trolleybuses which had been assembled in Leeds since late 1912. The redesign involved changing over to use Dick, Kerr & Co Ltd traction equipment and replacing the chain drive transmission with a new and improved chainless drive where each motor was geared to a rear wheel by one single reduction. The 'two basin'-type rear axles were supplied by Kirkstall Forge, another Leeds engineering company. After the previous body supplier, Milnes-Voss, closed its Birkenhead works in 1913.

Below:
The first seven trolleybuses to be fitted with bodies designed by C. H. Roe were supplied by RET Construction Co Ltd to Shanghai Electric Construction Co in 1914. Although the first ones had chain drive, at least one seen here inside the Balm Road Works was fitted with double-basin worm-driven Kirkstall axles. *RET/GLC*

Charles H. Roe designed a lightweight trolleybus body using teak for the framing braced with light steel sections and aluminium for the exterior lower panelling and shaped corners. This was the first of the Roe composite body designs which continued to be built until September 1968, when Northampton Corporation No 267 became the last composite body to be built by the Roe works.

These first composite bodies were built in Leeds by Lockwood & Clarkson whose works were on North Street, just north of the city centre.

RET Construction Co Ltd was able to test the completed trolleybuses on the Leeds Corporation route between the City and Farnley Moor Top.

When World War 1 began on 4 August 1914, a number of orders for new trolleybuses were under construction for Shanghai, Bloemfontein, and Ramsbottom, and the company was able to complete these by June 1915.

On 3 October 1914, Charles H. Roe, now 27 and resident at 5 North Terrace, Crossgates, married Kathleen Huxley, 25, of 12 Boughton, Chester at Newgate Street Presbyterian Church, Chester. After the wedding the couple moved to 'Rosemead', 58 Hollyshaw Lane, Whitkirk, less than half a mile south of Crossgates railway station, but outside the Leeds boundary.

As the war continued, the British Government quickly imposed restrictions under the Defence of the Realm Act 1914, where many established engineering companies became Government Controlled Establishments to utilise existing equipment and workforce to manufacture materials for the war effort. RET Construction Co Ltd became involved in the manufacture of munitions for the Ministry of Munitions and the National Shell Projectile factories.

On 3 July 1916, the company moved its London office to Leeds, and by 20 September 1916 the works were practically entirely engaged in war work. The company, unable to complete the order for North Ormesby, South Bank, Normanby & Grangetown Railless Traction Co, where four out of the 10 trolleybuses were nearly finished, was wound up voluntarily under wartime legislation on 29 January 1917. An Extraordinary General Meeting was held on 9 February 1917, followed by a Creditors Meeting on 26 February 1917, and the liquidator appointed was Alfred Page from 28 King Street, Cheapside, London.

The works, which were still fully occupied in the manufacture of 6in shell heads, were taken over in February 1917 by the Ministry of Munitions which paid rent to the liquidator for the whole of the premises, plant and equipment. The Ministry of Munitions ran the shops itself as a shell head producing factory until August 1917. In all, 35,492 shell heads were produced at 7s 5½d (37p) per head, a considerable reduction on the 8s 6d (42½p) per head being paid to other subcontractors.

By September 1917 the works were occupied by the Royal Flying Corps, possibly in connection with the Blackburn aeroplanes being built at Olympia in Roundhay, Leeds. The works were taken over in August 1919 by Leonard Cooper Ltd, structural steelwork engineers (who are still there).

Below:
The last trolleybuses to be completed by RET were the two metal-framed ones supplied to Ramsbottom Urban District Council in June 1915, again with C. H. Roe-designed bodies built by Lockwood & Clarkston in Leeds. *RET/GLC*

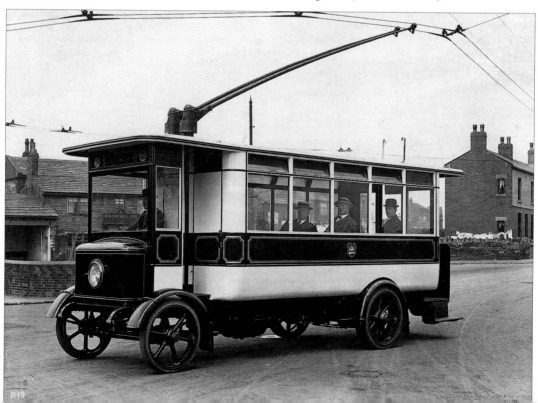

2. Charles H. Roe, Engineer and Jobbing Coach Builder, Balm Road Mills, 1917-20

During the war, Charles H. Roe was exempt from military service as he was a mechanical engineer and considerably skilled draughtsman, both of which were reserved occupations under the 1914 Defence of the Realm Act. He remained at the RET works until either February or possibly August 1917. However, we do know that sometime in 1917 he was first listed as an engineer and manufacturer of road and light rail bodies at Balm Road Mills, Hunslet. (Telegraphic address: Vehicles; Telephone number: 4832 Central.) This was the same address as the RET works, but was based in a different building which appears to have been previously occupied by W. D. Oddy & Co, manufacturers of aircraft propellers.

Charles H. Roe continued to be involved in war work as a subcontractor making gun carriages, hand carts, horse-drawn wagons and horse-drawn living vans for construction gangs.

On 25 September 1917, Charles H. Roe applied to Leeds City Council for consent to erect a temporary wood shed, followed by an application in March 1918 for a timber drying shed. On the day the war ended, 11 November 1918, Charles H. Roe (Engineer and Manufacturer) submitted an application for a patent for improvements in or relating to pulleys or driving drums.

Above left:
Roe bodybuilder's plate used in period 1917-20.

Below:
Amongst the early products built by C. H. Roe, Engineer and Manufacturer, were numerous heavy duty trailers suitable for use with steam-driven vehicles being built by the numerous steam road haulage manufacturers in Leeds such as Mann, Yorkshire, Fowler and McLaren. These trailers were built with a variety of bodies ranging from flat platform as shown here to side tipping wagons, some being divided into compartments for individual loads of materials such as coal which may have needed to be delivered to different places. *Roe*

As Britain slowly returned to producing articles required in peacetime, Charles H. Roe began building bodies for charabancs, vans and motor lorries as well as further horse-drawn wagons of all types. On 30 June 1919, Charles H. Roe (Engineer and Manufacturer) submitted a joint application with Thomas Tate, a Wakefield motor engineer, for a multiple tip-wagon for motor lurries [sic], which was designed to tip sideways individual loads of materials such as coal which may have to be delivered to different places.

The demand for new bodies meant further applications for extensions to his premises at Balm Road Mills. These included the building of a temporary wooden shed and covered way in November 1919, which enabled him to build bodies up to a maximum height of 12ft in a building 40ft wide and 60ft long.

One of the first bodies completed in these extensions was a special motor pantechnicon body built on a Leyland 4-ton chassis which was completed in February 1920 for J. Bullock & Sons Ltd, the well-known transport company based in Wakefield and Featherstone.

The works were kept busy with orders for reupholstery, repainting and repairing of all types of motor bodies, and quickly became well known to the carrying trades as builders of every type of motor body for both pleasure and commercial use.

Meanwhile, the goodwill and patents for the RET Construction Co Ltd had been sold by the receiver to Railless Ltd in spring 1918. Railless was a new company owned by Short Bros (Rochester & Bedford) Ltd, and manufacturing was transferred to that company's Seaplane Works in Rochester, Kent. Mr E. M. Munro continued to work for the new company.

The 10 outstanding trolleybuses for North Ormesby, South Bank, Normanby & Grangetown Railless Traction Co were finally completed after the war, and were delivered in August 1919. It is possible that Charles H. Roe was the subcontractor who finished the partially built ones. In late 1920, Railless Ltd supplied four one-man-operated trolleybuses to York Corporation fitted with 24-seat bodies. Mr Munro's other engineering assistant, Mr A. S. Crosley, stated that the bodywork was subcontracted to Roe, whilst Railless claimed in July 1922 that it had built them. Whether this is correct or not, it must be noted that all these vehicles bear a very strong resemblance to the bodies supplied to Ramsbottom in 1915, which had been designed by Charles H. Roe.

Below:
Typical of many of the small tradesman vehicle bodies built at Balm Road on a Ford Model T chassis is this mobile shop selling fresh fish door-to-door. In this case, the fish was despatched to Leeds by rail from Grimsby for distribution by road. U 7992 was new in 1920. *Roe*

Above:
This left-hand drive Ford Model T long-wheelbase chassis was fitted with a 12-seat charabanc body. The builder's plate on the windscreen frame proclaims body No 222 built by Roe, Balm Road Mills, which suggests that it was built before May 1920 when Charles H. Roe Ltd was formed. The driver is Mr Charles Henry Roe and the gentleman at the rear nearside may be his father, Charles Roe. *Roe*

Right:
September 1917 plan of Balm Road plan.

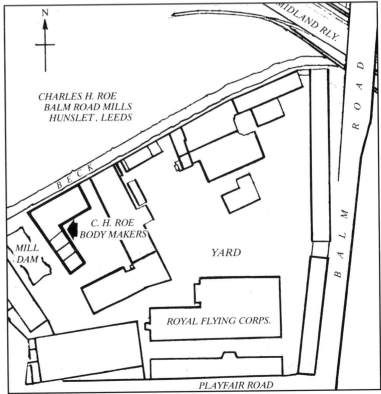

CHARLES H. ROE
BALM ROAD MILLS
HUNSLET, LEEDS

C. H. ROE
BODY MAKERS

MILL
DAM

YARD

ROYAL FLYING CORPS.

PLAYFAIR ROAD

BECK

MIDLAND RLY.

BALM ROAD

N

3. Charles H. Roe Ltd, Balm Road Mills, 1920-1

With expansion at Balm Road Mills being impossible, Charles H. Roe began to look elsewhere for suitable property in which to develop his business.

Having lived in the Crossgates area since 1914, he was aware that the Barnbow No 1 Filling Factory, built by the Ministry of Munitions during the war, had been cleared of machinery and equipment by August 1919.

During 1918, the factory employed between 600 and 700 people, and had been despatching two or three full train loads of ammunition daily to the front. The factory was being supplied with components, materials and other items by many hundreds of subcontractors, and had therefore found it necessary to employ a large fleet of Army Service Corps motor lorries to collect and distribute them. Although some goods were despatched to Barnbow by canal, a constant stream of lorries collected these items from a transhipment depot at Woodlesford on the Aire & Calder Canal.

In order to maintain these motor lorries, a fully equipped garage had been built at the Crossgates end of the factory. This garage was also used as the base for the works passenger transport vehicles, stores vans and, of course, ambulance cars with lady chauffeurs supplied by the 'Women's Legion'.

The garage premises had been constructed on land belonging to Manston Grange and occupied a 3-acre part of an 8-acre 24-perch plot of land known as Gate Close. Despite having a Crossgates, Leeds postal address, all the Barnbow site was actually in the Tadcaster RDC, part of the West Riding of Yorkshire.

On 3 May 1920, Charles H. Roe purchased the land, workshops, sheds and other buildings known as 'Crossgates Motor Works' from Frederick Ben Atkinson, a motor engineer who lived in Folkestone. The solicitor acting for the transaction was Alfred James Appleton of Leeds.

Atkinson had owned the land since 1898 and the last occupant of the works was given as 'Umpleby', who in 1920 was in residence at Manston Grange, also owned by Atkinson.

Charles H. Roe paid £450 cash and also took over the two mortgage debts of £7,000 and £1,200. He then arranged for incorporated accountant Thomas Whitwell Dresser to act for him in the sale of the goodwill of his engineering business to a new company to be formed to continue this business as Charles H. Roe Ltd. The existing business was to be sold for £2,835 10s: £35 10s in cash and £2,800 by the allotment to Charles H. Roe or his nominees of 2,800 fully paid up ordinary shares at £1 each. These shares were to be numbered 3 to 2802.

For the purpose of stamp duty payable, the existing plant machinery, office furniture, fittings and stock in trade capable of manual delivery, all forming part of the purchase, were assessed at £4,954 6s 10d, and the effective date of the sale was to be 1 May 1920. The

Below:
Another charabanc body built at Balm Road was this 28-seat example mounted on a Karrier WDS chassis, registered U 8184 in 1920.

Above:
During March-April 1921, at least five 16-seat charabancs were supplied to various members of the Harrogate Motor and Carriage Owners Association. These were all painted in a cream and grey livery and were probably the last bodies to be built at Balm Road. This is one of the five, WR 7xxx.

new company was registered on 26 May 1920 with Charles Henry Roe of Rosemead, Hollyshaw Lane, Whitkirk, Leeds and Charles Roe of 6 East Mount Road, York each having one share. The secretary and bookkeeper for the company was Charles H. Roe's youngest sister, Dorothea Lily.

The nominal capital of the new company was to be £15,000 divided into 15,000 shares of £1 each, and the registered office was situated at Balm Road Mills, Hunslet in the city of Leeds. The Memorandum of Association stated that the company was established to carry on the business as motor body builders; motor, electrical and marine and general engineering; road and rail vehicle building and maintaining; steam, electric and petrol or oil-driven boat, barge and ship building and machining; haulage contractors; general wood-working and machinery, cabinet and furniture making; and general joinery, wood pulley making and patent specialities.

By 2 July 1920, a total of 5,800 shares had been allotted or paid for by cash, split as follows:

Charles H. Roe – 2,300
Charles Roe – 1,500
Hargreaves Brotherton – 500
Alfred and Hargreaves Brotherton jointly – 1,500

This allowed the new company to complete the purchase of the original business on 5 August 1920.

However, the company did not yet have sufficient capital to proceed, and Charles H. Roe was forced to turn to brother and sisters for help. Eldest sister Fanny Blacker, spinster; brother John Thomas, railway clerk; and Dorothea Lily, also the company's secretary and book-keeper, purchased 400, 75 and 25 shares respectively.

In 1914, his friend Hargreaves Brotherton, who lived at 7 Tranquility, Crossgates, just around the corner from North Terrace where Charles H. Roe lived, was now a technical chemist living at 'Thornleigh' in Ashton-upon-Mersey, Cheshire. Hargreaves Brotherton purchased a further 245 shares and jointly with Alfred Brotherton, a cashier, a further 600 shares. This meant that by 29 September 1920 the subscribed share capital was £7,145.

The register of deeds records the transfer of all the hereditaments of F. B. Atkinson to Charles H. Roe Ltd Balm Road Mills on 22 March 1921. At this point, the registered office was moved to Old Manston Lane, Crossgates near Leeds.

Available records show that an Extraordinary General Meeting of the new company took place at Hollyshaw Lane, Whitkirk on 8 April 1921 when a special resolution was passed regarding the number of directors of the company. It was agreed that there should be not less than two and no more than seven, with the qualification of a director being the holding of 500 shares. The first directors were therefore to be Charles Henry Roe, Charles Roe, and Hargreaves Brotherton, and each was to be regarded as a permanent director.

On 29 April 1921 the above was confirmed at a further Extraordinary General Meeting at Old Manston Lane.

4. Crossgates Motor Works, 1921-2

During April 1921 the move to Crossgates from Hunslet took place and this allowed the company to develop its motor engineering business. Charles H. Roe visited the London office of Railless Ltd on 18 April 1921 and agreed to supply three bodies to his design for the three trolleybuses ordered by Bloemfontein.

In late summer 1921, Railless Ltd subcontracted the bodies for the 12 double-deck trolleybuses ordered by Birmingham Corporation to Roe. As with the earlier trolleybuses built in Leeds, these vehicles were also tested there.

On 14 July 1921, a debenture for £7,000 was secured with the London County Westminster and Parrs Bank.

One of the companies which Charles H. Roe had been involved with whilst working for RET Construction Co Ltd was Clough, Smith & Co Ltd engineers and contractors, who had erected the overhead equipment for RET using Brecknell, Munro & Rogers Ltd supplied components. During 1921, Clough, Smith arranged for the manufacture of the Straker-Clough trolley omnibus and chose Roe to build the bodies for the first eight vehicles. The first vehicle was delivered to Teesside RTB in October 1921 and the second to Rotherham in May 1922.

By November 1921, Roe was placing 'poetic licence' advertisements that said:

Go to the Actual Builders – it Pays. If you specialise a ROE Body you obtain one that is guaranteed perfectly constructed by master craftsmen who have designed and built bodies for the world's largest transport users. ROE constructed bodies have been 'as good as ever' after years of continual hard service. Send us your enquiries for bus, charabanc and commercial bodies.

'Phone Crossgates 93' GRAMS: 'Vehicles, Leeds' Contractors to HM Government

Above:
Roe bodybuilder's transfer used at Crossgates Motor Body Works.

Below:
One of the first vehicles to be photographed outside Crossgates Motor Works is this Thornycroft J which is probably another ex-WD chassis. This time, the customer is one of the many Silver Motor Services.

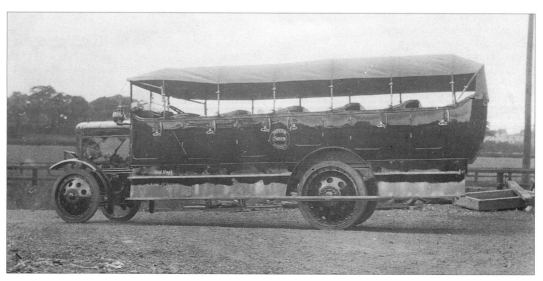

Other work being done was the painting and repair of bodies of all types, as well as building private motor car bodies on a variety of chassis.

Roe charabanc bodies, large and small, were supplied to many of the Leeds & District owners and the company was also chosen to build bodies by many of the members of the Harrogate Motor and Carriage Owners Association who favoured small light 14-seat coaches painted cream that were mounted on Fiat chassis shod with pneumatic tyres.

By 7 December 1921, the company secretary was George W. Myers who, when confirming that the number of shares issued was still 7,145, stated that a new director had been appointed. This was Henry Elsworth, an engineer from The Avenue, Scholes near Leeds.

Work on the Birmingham trolleybus order caused the company to secure another debenture of £3,000 on 31 December 1921 from the same bank.

On 5 September 1922, the bank appointed John Gordon as receiver of the property of Charles H. Roe Ltd. On 24 November 1922 at an Extraordinary General Meeting of the company, the following extra-ordinary resolution was passed: 'That it has been proved to the satisfaction of this meeting that the company cannot by reason of its liabilities continue its business.'

The company was to be wound up voluntarily and John Gordon be appointed liquidator.

The liquidator took responsibility for recovering the outstanding monies on and from 5 September 1922 until 20 January 1923. When John Gordon ceased to act as the receiver and liquidator on 3 June 1924 he had been able to realise the sum of £5,390 14s 2d which gave a surplus balance to the bank of £16 15s 2d. Some £3,133 3s 6d had been received for book debts plus a further £900 from Railless Ltd.

The assets of the old company were sold to C. H. Roe for £1,140. Eventually on 22 February 1929, the 1920 company was finally dissolved.

5. Charles H. Roe (1923) Ltd, Crossgates Motor Works, 1923-7

On 22 February 1923, a new company – Charles H. Roe (1923) Ltd – was registered with a share capital of £8,500. The first directors were Arthur Lambert Foster of Starbeck in the County of York and Charles Henry Roe, Engineer, of Crossgates in the County of York.

On 24 February 1923, the freehold premises of Crossgates Motor Works were acquired by Arthur Lambert Foster on behalf of the company, together with the goodwill of the business of motor engineers recently carried on by Charles H. Roe Ltd for £5,300. A further sum of £5,840 was paid for the stock in trade undisposed of on 20 January 1923.

The transaction was satisfied by a cash payment to C. H. Roe of £5,140 and the allotment of shares in the new company to the value of £6,000 to C. H. Roe or his nominees. At the first Board Meeting on 5 March 1923,

Above:
Roe bodybuilders' transfer used by the 1923 company.

Below:
The new 1923 company continued to supply many of the local operators with charabanc bodies on a variety of chassis. As the demand for bus services grew, Karrier Motors Ltd placed a contract with Roe for the supply of 20-seat saloon bus bodies for its CY model chassis. With Karrier selling the complete vehicle it is not often realised that these were Roe bodies and it is known that the four supplied to Manchester Corporation in July 1923 were identical to ones known to have been built at Crossgates, such as this one, WT 3872, supplied in May 1924 to Premier Transport Co, Keighley. However, by then, the CY chassis was available with pneumatic-tyred wheels on the front axle whilst retaining solid-tyred rear wheels. In September 1924, Karrier Motors complained that a recent body was not up to standard.

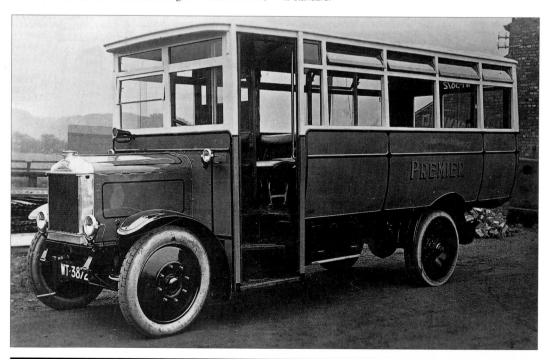

further directors were appointed, so that the Board now consisted of:

Chairman
Arthur Lambert Foster, Harrison Hill House, Starbeck, Harrogate, Director of Chemicals Aerated Mineral Waters Ltd (CAMWAL) Starbeck. Director of Fletchers Sauce Company, Selby. Councillor from 1920 in Starbeck Ward at Harrogate.

Managing Director
Charles Henry Roe, Engineer.

Directors
John Thomas Roe – clerk, North Eastern Railway
Ellis Franklin – rainwear manufacturer, Leeds
Director & Company Secretary
Edward Warwick Broadbent – chartered accountant

A total of £8,000 in shares had been issued and the maximum number of directors was to be five. On 20 April 1923, a mortgage to secure all monies due or to become due from the company to Westminster Bank Ltd was obtained.

The Objects for which the Company is established are:

To carry on the businesses of Carriage Builders, Motor Body Builders, Motor, Electrical, Marine and General Engineers, Road and Rail Vehicle Builders and Maintainers, Trackless Tram Makers, Builders and Maintainers of Steam, Electric and Petrol or Oil-driven Boats, Barges, and Ships, Motor Garage Proprietors, Haulage Contractors, General Wood Workers and Machinists, Cabinet, Furniture, and Packing Case Makers and General Joiners, Wood Pulley Makers, and Makers of Patent Specialities.

During 1923 the first orders were received for motorbus bodies to be fitted to motorbus chassis being supplied to municipalities. Probably the first one to be completed was for Ramsbottom UDC on a Thornycroft chassis, which was followed by three bodies for fitting onto Bristol 2-ton chassis for Rotherham. At that time, many of the customers ordered a complete vehicle from the chassis supplier, and, in the case of Rotherham, it might just be a coincidence that Bristol-based Mr E. M. Munro left Railless in June 1923 to resume his independent consultancy practice.

One of the companies which sold complete vehicles to the municipalities wanting to experiment with the use of motorbuses to feed its existing tramway system was Tramway Supplies Ltd, Grove Mills in Meanwood, Leeds. They in turn subcontracted the order for the chassis to a well known manufacturer and also arranged for the Blackburn Aeroplane and Motor Co Ltd, whose works were at Olympia, Roundhay, Leeds to build the body. Huddersfield Corporation therefore purchased Karrier and Guy buses from Tramway Supplies with Blackburn-built bodies. Other municipalities supplied with Blackburn-bodied vehicles were Chesterfield, Colne, Derby and Lytham St Annes and the last

Blackburn bodies appear to have been completed in July 1924.

An interesting story surrounds the building of the Tilling-Stevens Petrol Electric Railless Chassis I (PERC I) built to the design patented by Mr J. B. Parker, the TRTB General Manager. Tilling-Stevens subcontracted the bodywork to Tramway Supplies, who in turn subcontracted it to Blackburn Aeroplane, who in turn subcontracted it to Charles H. Roe (1923) Ltd. In March 1924, Mr J. B. Parker wrote to Tramway Supplies: 'I intend to make an inspection of the new omnibus body which you are building for us.' When Parker sent a letter to the Chairman of the Teesside RT Board, Mr W. G. Grace, it contained the statement, 'I inspected the manufacture of the new body at Crossgates, Leeds on Saturday last', which makes it difficult for historians and researchers to get it right!

During late 1923, Roe rebuilt the bodies on five of the Dodson-bodied Cedes-Stoll trolleybuses for Keighley Corporation. The work involved removing the rear entrance and platforms as well as modifying the bodies to front entrance for use as 'one-man' vehicles, at a cost of £60 for each vehicle. During 1924, all five were remounted onto new Straker-Clough Trolley Omnibus chassis.

In 1924, the Derwent Valley Light Railway Co took delivery of a tandem-type railcar in which two ordinary Ford 1-ton chassis were fitted with special axles and wood-spoked wheels with steel tyres suitable for running on the standard gauge track. Each chassis was fitted with an 18-seat Roe-built body 7ft 3in wide with two entrances. The railcars operated over the 16-mile-long branch line with only the leading car being powered. The trailing car was left out of gear with the engine stationary. The total cost of these railcars was £1,070, and they were used until 1926 when passenger services ceased on the DVLR. The railcars were then sold to the County Donegal Joint Railway Committee where they were adapted and converted to run on their 3ft gauge lines.

Many operators now realised that the charabanc business was dependent upon the weather, which was not reliable, and it could therefore be more profitable to run all year round services using buses fitted with saloon bodies. This meant that by 1925, Roe had quite a large stock of secondhand charabanc bodies, having replaced them with new saloon bodies.

By this time, the works had a total floor space of 27,000sq ft, and it was expected that extensions would have to be built in the near future to cope with the demand for bodies.

In July 1925, the prototype Garrett trolleybus chassis type 'S', bodied by Roe, was tested in Leeds, Keighley and Bradford.

Straker-Squire Ltd, the supplier of the basic chassis for the Straker, Clough Trolley Omnibus, was voluntarily liquidated on 12 May 1925, and the new company of the same name had to call in the official receiver on 16 July 1926. Clough, Smith had a supply problem. From available records, it is known that from the summer of 1925 until the end of May 1927, Clough,

Smith & Co Ltd rented buildings from C. H. Roe (1923) Ltd at Crossgates, Leeds, paying a substantial amount in rent. What is not clear is what the buildings, comprising one body shop and the paint shop, were used for. The period involved is concurrent with the Straker-Squire difficulties and one is left to speculate whether Straker-Clough chassis had the electrical equipment fitted there.

On 15 December 1925, a debenture for £2,000 with a charge of 6% interest was agreed with the Westminster Bank Ltd, and, on 26 July 1926, a further debenture for £300 was raised against its property including uncalled capital, again with the Westminster Bank. A further £900 was raised again on the property and uncalled capital on 27 July 1926; this time the person entitled to the charge was Charles Henry's mother, Mrs Elizabeth Roe, now a widow in York.

The capital raised from the debentures enabled the company to purchase the remaining portion of Gate Close together with part of the adjoining field on the east boundary. This now gave the company a site with an area of 9 acres 9 perches, of which nearly 6 acres were used for the company's bodybuilding activities whilst the remaining 3 acres were used for the small house, 'Fairfield' built for Mr and Mrs C. H. Roe, which they occupied until 1938, and the 'Home Farm' which was used to raise the annual 'bird' despatched to the home address of managers, etc, during December each year.

Additional buildings were erected to form the new body shop, and in September 1926, the company advertised for a works manager to look after day-to-day production. The successful applicant was Mr William Bramham, who had previously been at Crossgates as a draughtsman, and before that had worked for a Leeds engineering company.

Many of the bus bodies built by Blackburn Aeroplane & Motor Co were mounted on Guy Motors Ltd 30cwt or 2-ton chassis suitable for 16-20-seat bodywork. It is known that after July 1924, Roe built a very similar body on a Guy 30cwt chassis which may have been the one demonstrated to Leeds City Tramways during 1925.

During the summer of 1926, Leeds City Tramways' manager carried out tests with three motorbuses from different manufacturers. One of these was an Albion PK26 29-seat bus which was demonstrated during August. This vehicle was fitted with a Roe body with rear entrance, and was registered GD 4265. It was eventually purchased by Hebble Motor Services in March 1927. Leeds must have been impressed with the bodywork, as in December 1926 they ordered their first 12 Roe bodies for mounting on Karrier Motors Ltd normal control chassis. When they were delivered in February-March 1927 the Yorkshire Post reported on 22 March that: 'Leeds was very satisfied with the Roe bodies and hoped their use by the city would have the effect of encouraging other local authorities to place business with the Leeds firm.'

The expansion of the production facilities at Crossgates was justified with an increase in the number of bodies being built, some 47 being completed in 1926. This increased to 70 in 1927 and 66 in 1928.

The types of bodies being built also changed, with demand for motorbus bodies overtaking orders for trolleybus bodies which totalled 32 in 1926, but had fallen to 11 by 1928. During the same period orders for motorbus bodies had risen from 15 in 1926 to 55 in 1928.

Below:
The first orders for motorbus bodies known to have been placed direct by municipalities were from Ramsbottom UDC in September 1923 and these were followed by one from Rotherham Corporation for three Bristol type 'O' 2-ton chassis, completed in late 1923. Two of these, ET 2795 and 2796, pose outside the works before being despatched to Rotherham. During the next four years, many other customers had Bristols bodied by Roe.

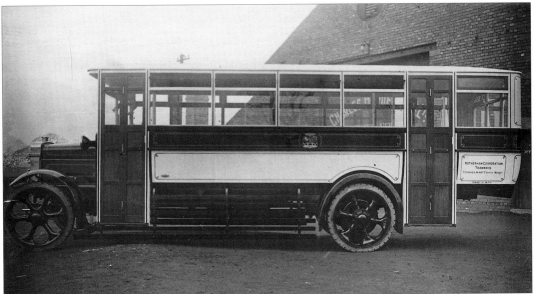

Top:
Northampton Corporation Omnibuses purchased four Thornycroft A1 chassis fitted with 16-seat bodies. Northampton records state that Nos 9 and 10 were bodied by York, Ward & Rowlatt Ltd, the Thornycroft dealer in Northampton in October 1924. However, the photographs of 9 and 10 show a body-builder's transfer on the side panels adjacent to the door. While interior photographs of No 9 show that a bodybuilders' transfer was applied above the rear emergency door which states 'Coachwork by Chas H. Roe Ltd Leeds'. No 9, one of the first pair, is seen photographed in Northampton when new. The second pair bodied by Roe arrived in August 1925 and were numbered 11 and 12.

Above:
Rotherham Corporation purchased six Bristol 4-ton chassis fitted with 32-seat dual-doored Roe bodies. The first three were fitted with solid-tyred wheels and delivered between late 1924 and early 1925, while the last three ran on pneumatic tyres. ET 3216, Rotherham No 75, is seen here at Crossgates.

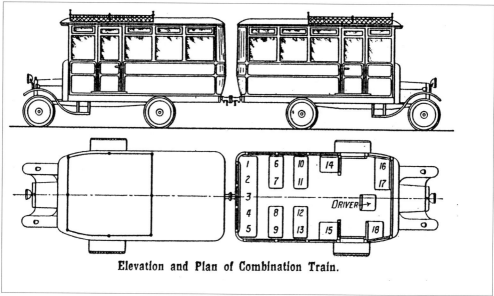

Elevation and Plan of Combination Train.

Top:
When the Derwent Valley Light Railway, like many other under-takings, faced competition from small bus companies in the early 1920s, it introduced, in late 1924, a tandem-type Ford railcar in an effort to cut operating costs. The railcar comprised two separate units coupled together back to back. Each chassis was a standard Ford 1-ton truck with an 18-seat body built by Charles H. Roe (1923) Ltd. The pair are seen at the

York Layerthorpe station of the DVLR and the wood-spoked wheels and light steel tyres show how light the unit was, with each car weighing just over 2 tons. The petrol consumed was 14.33mpg, and if only one car was run, it rose to 17.55mpg. *Courtesy NRM Collection*

Above:
Elevation and plan of combination train.

Right:
Even the use of these economical railcars failed to make the DVLR passenger services financially viable, so in late 1926 passenger service ceased. The two redundant railcars were sold to the County Donegal Joint Railway Committee in North West Ireland where the manager, Mr Curran, adapted and modified them to run on the 3ft gauge system. One of the modified cars is seen at Stranorlar with the Roe body now being low enough for passengers to board at wayside halts without platforms and at level crossings. *Courtesy NRM Collection*

Below:
In 1925 Doncaster Corporation placed its first three double-deck motorbuses into service. These vehicles had 50-seat Roe bodies mounted on AEC type 504 chassis. They were numbered 50-2, WT 9712, WT 9078 and WU 2089 and No 51 was the first one to be delivered in March 1925. The seating arrangement on delivery was 24 seats on the upper deck and 26 seats on the lower deck, as seen in the original of this photograph on the platform side of the rear bulkhead of the lower saloon.

Above:
Doncaster Corporation also placed three single-deck AEC type 503 motorbuses with 30-seat forward-entrance Roe bodies into service in 1925. Numbered 14-16, WU 484, 483 and 2676, this photograph shows No 15 when new in May 1925.

Below:
Roe built a 20-seat body on this Thornycroft A1 chassis for the Lake District Road Traffic Co, Keswick. The LDRTC was taken over by Lancashire & Westmorland in July 1925, who were taken over in turn by Ribble Motor Services in December 1927. EC 5858, new in 1924, did not pass to Ribble in December 1927.

Above right:
Mexborough & Swinton Tramways Co purchased two Dennis 4-ton chassis fitted with Roe dual-door bodies which seated 26 passengers and entered service in June 1925, numbered 32 and 33. No 33, WU 1508, is seen outside Crossgates prior to despatch.

Below right:
The prototype Garrett type S trolleybus was fitted with a Roe 32-seat centre-entrance body and was demonstrated to Leeds, Keighley and Bradford Corporations in early July 1925. It then went to Ipswich until March 1926. The Garrett was then purchased by Bradford Corporation in October 1927 after having been on loan since February 1927 during which time it had been converted to pneumatic-tyred wheels.

Above:

Between the summer of 1925 and the end of May 1927, Clough, Smith & Son Ltd rented buildings from C. H. Roe (1923) Ltd at Crossgates. These buildings comprised one body shop and the paint shop; however it is unclear what they were used for. The period involved is concurrent with difficulties with the chassis supplier and it is believed that the Straker-Clough chassis had the electrical equipment fitted there. Twenty-eight out of the 54 chassis built in this period had Roe bodies. The 24 for Darlington Corporation on solid-tyred chassis were delivered between December 1925 and September 1926, and fleet No 7 is seen in early 1926 being tested in Darlington. The remaining four Roe-bodied vehicles had pneumatic tyres and were low loading (LL) models delivered to Rotherham Corporation. *BTH/GLC*

Above right:

Oldham Corporation placed its first eight double-deck motorbuses into service in February 1926. Numbered 10-17 they were registered BU 3991-3998. The AEC type 507 chassis were fitted with Roe 52-seat bodies similar to the ones supplied to Doncaster in 1925 and had 26 seats in both saloons. The first one to be completed, Oldham 12, is seen at Crossgates.

Right:

In June 1926, Teesside Railless Traction Board acquired its first motorbus which had a 26-seat body built by Roe mounted on a Daimler CM chassis. PY 5573 was given fleet No 23 and was incorrectly lettered with a speed limit of 20mph rather than 12mph when photographed. The vehicle was legally restricted to 12mph due to being fitted with solid tyres rather than pneumatics.

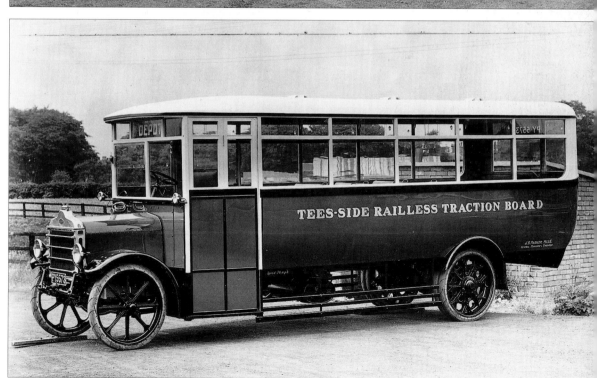

Left and below:

In November 1926, Oldham placed a further three double-deck motorbuses into service, numbered 18-20 and registered BU 4509-4511. They were again bodied by Roe, this time with 50-seat bodies fitted onto normal-control Guy BX chassis. While the overall length was slightly longer than the earlier AEC examples the driver was sat in the lower saloon, hence there were only 24 seats in the lower saloon.

6. Crossgates Carriage Works, 1927-34

During late 1927, the name of the works was changed from Crossgates Motor Works to Crossgates Carriage Works.

One of the most recognisable features on many of the bodies built at Crossgates was the 2¾in deep waistrail moulding which projected ⅝in outwards. The moulding was part of a waistrail machined to shape from a 4⅛in x 2in piece of teak which included the special pillar joints, and was first used in about 1924.

In early 1928, an application was made in the joint names of Charles H. Roe (1923) Ltd, Charles Henry Roe and William Bramham to the Patents Office for an invention relating to improvements in or relating to 'Waist Rail and Pillar Joints in Vehicle Body Construction'. In June 1929 the complete specification was accepted and patented as No 313720. This patent became one of the key features of the Roe standard composite body.

In February 1929, Charles H. Roe (1923) Ltd entered into an agreement with Alfred Marsden Alcock from Wigan. The agreement allowed Roe to build under licence double-deck bus bodies with both a rear stair-case for access to the top deck and a front staircase as a means of exit from the top deck to the front exit doorway. Roe was licensed to build and sell bodies of this type to existing customers comprising Mexborough & Swinton and 13 municipalities. The licence also stated that Massey Bros was excluded from supplying these 14 customers. In 1933, Roe built six dual-door double-deck buses to Alcock's patent for Bury Corporation, which was not one of the 14. In 1929, six demonstration Crossley Eagle chassis were bodied at Crossgates for Crossley Motors Ltd, one of these being fitted with a double-deck body which was only 13ft 6in high. The upper deck had a sunken gangway on both sides of the vehicle, and the two rows of seats were in a herringbone formation facing half forward down the centre of the upper deck.

Another achievement in 1929 was the building of a number of coach bodies for the West Yorkshire Road Car Co at Harrogate, where, incidentally, the Roe Chairman, Alderman Arthur Lambert Foster was the Mayor in 1931-2.

During 1930, Ellis Franklin ceased to be a director after selling his shares, while Hargreaves Brotherton, a chemical manufacturer from Ashton-on-Mersey, joined the Board. Brotherton had been one of the original 1920 company directors.

In August 1930, Mr J. C. Whiteley, the General Manager and Engineer of Grimsby Corporation Tramways, took delivery of an AEC double-deck bus with a new type of body he had designed to facilitate the rapid loading and unloading of passengers on busy routes. The wide central entrance allowed access to the two lower saloons and to the two staircases leading to the upper deck. The bus, seating 48 passengers, had 25 seats on the upper deck.

On 11 August 1930, a joint patent application was made in the names of C. H. Roe (1923) Ltd, C. H. Roe and John Christopher Whiteley for this centre-entrance double-deck bus design. This patent, No 352295, was granted on 9 July 1931.

Meanwhile, on 25 February 1930, another similar application had been made by The English Electric Co Ltd and Walter Gray Marks for a patent for the five AEC Regents fitted with English Electric centre-entrance bodies built for Nottingham Corporation in early 1930. This patent, No 353483, was granted on 27 July 1931 and immediately English Electric complained to the Patent Office that the Whiteley patent infringed theirs. All this led to a hearing in July 1932 when both patents were ruled to infringe earlier patents going back to 1892, 1912 and 1913. The outcome was that both the Roe and the English Electric patents were allowed after amendment. At this point, both Roe and EE agreed that each patent holder was entitled to half of the royalty payment from any other manufacturer building centre-entrance double-deck bodies. This meant Brush, Burlingham and Weymann all paid £10 per vehicle, which was shared out £5 to EE, £2 10s to J. C. Whiteley, and the balance being divided between the Roe company, C. H. Roe and W. Bramham.

Incidentally, in October 1931 Leyland Motors Ltd had to apologise to the Grimsby manager after one of their representatives had inspected the new type of double-deck bus body without Mr Whiteley's consent. Leyland's letter said that the representative was sent to

Grimsby to ride on the bus in service as a paying passenger in order to find out how it compared with rear-entrance double-deck buses. It was not in any way with a view to obtaining particulars and dimensions as to its construction.

The early 1930s saw many new customers ordering bodies from Crossgates. These included the BEF companies, County Motors, Yorkshire Woollen District and Yorkshire Traction, as well as the important inde-pendent companies, Lancashire United Transport and its parent company, South Lancashire Transport which purchased 46 Roe bodies for its first tram replacement trolleybuses. When the West Riding tramcars were replaced by 50 motorbuses, they had centre-entrance double-deck bodies built at Crossgates.

On 27 January 1934, the shares belonging to Alderman Lambert Foster were sold and C. H. Roe became Chairman and Managing Director.

Above:
Grimsby Corporation placed six Albion PM28 motorbuses into service in December 1927, fleet Nos 21-6, registered EE 7411-6. The centre-entrance 32-seat bodies were built by Roe and were of similar layout to the Garrett trolleybuses supplied with Roe bodies in 1926-7.

Below:
Some of the last Roe bodies built in 1927 were the four 32-seat front-entrance vehicles fitted on Bristol B chassis supplied in December to Williamson's Garage Ltd, Heanor in Derbyshire, registered RA 4516-9.

Above:
During 1928 Leeds City Tramways & Transport Department purchased 12 large-capacity single-deck buses, all of which were three-axle. Karrier Motors supplied eight on WL6 chassis and Guy Motors supplied the other four on FCX chassis. Roe fitted 40-seat bodies to the Karriers; however the Guys were heavier and therefore had 38-seat bodies. Guy No 63 UM 8083 is seen here in July 1928.

Below:
One of the exhibits at the Municipal Tramways Conference in September 1928 in Manchester was a demonstration bus displayed by Albion Motors Ltd, who had arranged for Roe to build a 32-seat body on a PM28 chassis. This was eventually registered CN 3779 and was sold to General County Omnibus Co, County Durham. This was the second Albion demonstrator to have been fitted with a Roe body; the earlier one, GD 4265, had been built in early 1926.

Left:
Crossley Motors Ltd contracted Roe to build a total of six bodies for demonstration vehicles. VR 88 was the most unusual, being fitted with a 13ft 6in-high double-deck body built on a strengthened 'Eagle' single-deck chassis. The upper deck was provided with a wide gangway all round the 24 seats which are mounted back-to-back down the centre of the upper saloon, and 27 passengers were accommodated in the lower saloon. The vehicle was sold to Blumer's Motors Ltd, Greatham.

Left:
Another type of body built at Crossgates was the rear-entrance front-exit 32-seat body, in this case on a Karrier JKL chassis. No 18 was one of two supplied to York Corporation in September 1928.

Below left:
Leeds City Tramways & Transport Department was one of the first customers to purchase Crossley Eagle motorbus chassis when it was introduced in 1928. Four were placed into service in January 1929, all with 32-seat Roe bodywork, numbered 74-7. No 74 had a front entrance whilst the other three had rear entrances with the Scottish type cutaway rear panel and an entrance step similar to a double-deck bus. One of these, No 75, is seen when new in January 1929.

Right:
Patent waistrail.

Below:
When Gloucester Corporation started operating motorbuses in September 1929, it purchased four Thornycroft-type BC Forward-type chassis fitted with Roe 32-seat single-deck bodies with cutaway rear-entrance platforms, similar to the Leeds Crossley shown on page 30. No 11, FH 6180, is seen when new.

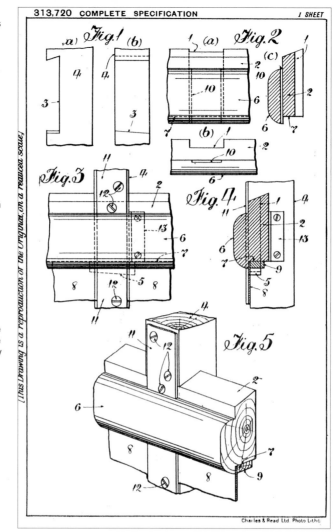

Above:
When vehicles became reliable enough to warrant the introduction of long-distance services linking Yorkshire to London, both West Yorkshire Road Car Co Ltd from Harrogate and Yorkshire Woollen District from Dewsbury placed new Leyland Tiger TS2 motorbuses into service fitted with Roe front-entrance bodies seating 26 on coach seats. One of the February 1930 examples supplied to West Yorkshire, No 516 WX 2102, clearly shows the semi-bucket-type coach seats.

Below:
Rotherham Corporation was unusual in owning two Roe-bodied coaches mounted on Bristol B chassis. These were used for 'private party work' and Roe records list each as a '28-seat De Luxe saloon bus'. ET 6224 Rotherham 110 was new in June 1930.

Above:
Building bodies for trolleybuses continued to be undertaken at Crossgates. This view of Bloemfontein No 5 on a Karrier-Clough trolley omnibus chassis, and South Lancashire Transport Co No 1, one of 10, on Guy BTX chassis, allows comparison of driving positions. Both chassis have three axles and are 28ft long, with the SLT ones being lowbridge examples and the Karrier still having an upper deck which did not extend over the driving cab.

Right:
When Grimsby Corporation placed an AEC Regent motorbus No 38 EE 9860 into service in August 1930 it was claimed to be the first centre-entrance double-deck bus to be built in Britain. Its 48-seat Roe body with twin staircases from the centre entrance to the upper deck had been built to the designs of the Grimsby manager, J. C. Whiteley. However, Nottingham Corporation's manager, W. G. Marks, had designed a centre-entrance double-deck bus and had already placed five in service some months earlier with English Electric-built bodies with a single staircase, also on AEC chassis. With both patent applications pending approval, both companies found that earlier patents had been infringed and amended specifications after litigation gave equal patent rights to Roe and English Electric who shared the royalty payments from other bodybuilders. Interestingly, in 1922 Blackburn Aeroplane & Motor Co Ltd had built a centre-entrance double-deck trolleybus body on a Trackless Car chassis which was operated by Leeds Corporation from 1924 until 1927.

BODY BY
CHAS. H. **ROE** 1923 LTD.
CROSSGATES
LEEDS
PHONE: X GATES 83 GRAMS: VEHICLES

LEEDS

EMERGENCY EXIT

104

Crossley

UA-5854

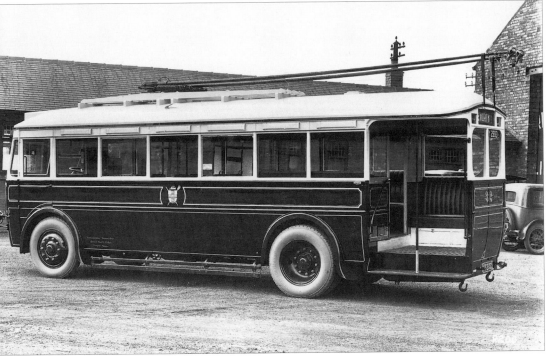

Left:
In November 1930, Leeds City Tramways & Omnibus Department placed six double-deck motorbuses into service, two on Leyland Titan TD1 chassis and four on Crossley Condor chassis. All six had Roe bodies with emergency doors fitted to the lower saloon offside as shown in this view of No 104 UA 5854, one of the Crossleys.

Top:
In January 1931, one of a batch of 10 Leyland LT2 single-deck buses with Roe 30-seat bodies was photographed at Crossgates before despatch to Lancashire United Transport & Power Co Ltd. The vehicles, allocated fleet numbers 206-15, were registered TF 3575-84.

Above:
The only single-deck Karrier-Clough trolley omnibuses to be built were three supplied with Roe 32-seat rear-entrance bodies with open platforms, Nos 30-2 VY 2991-3, to York Corporation in September 1931. They were the last new vehicles to be bought by York Corporation, which sold all its services to York-West Yorkshire Joint Committee on 1 April 1934. The trolleybuses were withdrawn on 6 January 1935 and then sold to Chesterfield Corporation.

Above left:
Middlesbrough Corporation No 50, XG 1192, was one of four Daimler CH6 model double-deck motorbuses fitted with Roe 52-seat bodies. Unlike similar vehicles supplied to Doncaster and York, these were supplied with the aluminium side panels unpainted, although the window surrounds and roof were painted white and the horizontal beadings and waist rail black. The vehicles were completed in 1931.

Left:
Another new customer to receive buses in 1931 with Roe bodies was Burnley Corporation which purchased four single-deck AEC Regals and eight double-deck AEC Regents. The double-deck bodies were built to the same design as Grimsby No 38.

Top:
In 1933, Doncaster Corporation purchased a Dennis Lancet single-deck bus with a 32-seat Roe body. Numbered 43, it was registered DT 4148 and remained in service until late 1942.

Above:
Oldham Corporation placed its first diesel-engined buses in service in 1933. Amongst them were nine Leyland Tiger TS4 single-deck motorbuses with Roe 32-seat bodies. Numbered 21-9, they were registered BU 7608-16. One of these, No 24, is seen at Crossgates.

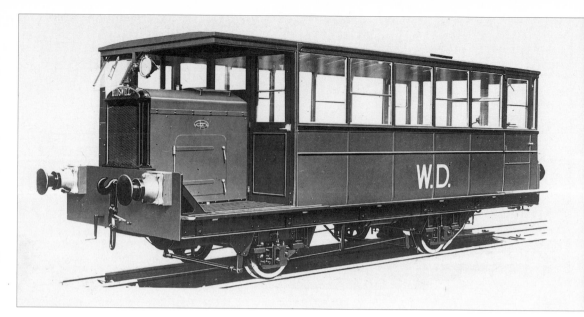

Above:
To service the Spurn Point lighthouse and naval installations, a 3½-mile standard gauge railway was built in 1910 to connect Kilnsea Fort with Spurn Point, and various forms of motive power were used. For the passenger service run for personnel, the Director of Army Contracts ordered a 30hp four-wheel standard gauge car on a 10ft wheelbase chassis built by Hudswell Clarke & Co Ltd powered by a Dorman four-cylinder engine. A 20-seat body was built by Roe, and the total cost of the railcar was £932 10s. It was delivered to the Spurn & Kilnsea Railway on 3 August 1933.
Photograph courtesy Ronald N. Redman, Collection

Below:
AEC arranged for Roe to build a centre-entrance body on one of the new Q type 761 demonstration chassis registered in London as AML 663 for the CM Show in November 1933. The vehicle was in the livery of Grimsby Corporation and numbered 48 in its fleet whilst on hire to Grimsby, who eventually purchased it.

Above:
Leeds City Transport Department in March 1934 placed a new AEC Regent into service fitted with an all-metal framed body built by Roe using framing supplied by Metal Sections – it was numbered 63, UG 8779. It enabled Leeds to compare it with the metal-framed bodies previously supplied by English Electric and Metropolitan Cammell Weymann. The style and shape of the body was influenced by W. Vane Morland and was similar to the ones supplied in late 1932 to his specification which included the slight vee formation to the upper-deck front windows.

Left:
Oldham Corporation purchased an experimental Crossley Mancunian double-deck bus in May 1934 fitted with a Roe H28/25R body. It was numbered 57, BU 7945. While the external appearance was practically identical to the Leeds AEC No 63, the composite body construction and heavier oil engine meant that the seating capacity was 53 instead of 56 in order to comply with the maximum permissible weight allowed at that time.

Above and right:
In December 1933 Wallasey Corporation Motors ordered 11 new buses for delivery in 1934. The chassis order was split, with AEC supplying 10 and Leyland one. The body orders were also unusual. English Electric supplied six AEC Regents with dual-staircase bodies, while Roe supplied centre-entrance bodies with twin staircases on a Leyland Titan TD3C – No 92 HF 9381 – in August 1934, two AEC Regents in May 1934 and two AEC Q types in July 1934. One of the two AEC Q buses, No 102 HF 9401, is seen in service.

7. Charles H. Roe Ltd, 1934-47

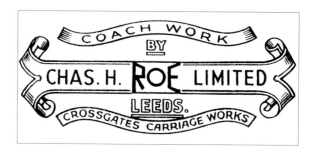

On 21 June 1934, an Extraordinary General Meeting of the (1923) company passed the following special resolutions:

1. That the name of the company be changed to Charles H. Roe Ltd.
2. That the maximum number of directors be increased from five to seven.

These were followed by the passing of one extraordinary resolution allowing the company to increase its share capital from £8,500 to £12,000, to be divided into 10,000 ordinary shares of £1 each and 2,000 6% cumulative preference shares of £1 each.

During November of that year, the three outstanding mortgages or charges were paid back and then a first-mortgage debenture of £15,000 was lodged with the bank. On 1 January 1935 the Works Manager Mr William Bramham became a director.

During early 1935, the Leeds manager William Vane Morland, concerned about the number and cost of staircase accidents, was inspired to sketch out a staircase with two landings which completely eliminated those costly insurance claims.

At the same time, AEC persuaded Roe to build a special streamlined double-deck bus for the Leeds City Transport exhibit on the Charles H. Roe stand for the CM Show at Olympia in November 1935. When the completed vehicle appeared, it created quite a stir. The body construction was entirely new. All the metal sections had been formed and fabricated in the Roe works, and the construction was so arranged that none of the bolts or rivets was stressed. The design of the skeleton framework and its construction was patented in the joint names of Charles H. Roe Ltd and William Bramham, while the new safety staircase designed by William Vane Morland was incorporated into the body design and this was patented in the joint names of Charles H. Roe Ltd, William Bramham and William Vane Morland. This staircase incorporated two ample passing platforms for passengers and was arranged to give a lot more space on the platform for the conductor as well as moving the bottom step of the staircase farther away from the platform edge. This type of staircase became known as the 'Roe safety staircase', and some 777 double-deck bodies were built before the

patent rights expired on 31 October 1950. By then, the staircase design had been modified to suit the modern trend for large seating capacity vehicles, so that the design had only a slight resemblance to its former layout. One modification was the fitting of a double-step entrance to the rear platform. As well as giving a flat floor into the saloon, it allowed the double landing staircase to protrude less into the upper saloon, allowing another row of seats to be fitted in the upper saloon after the increase in length of double-deck buses from 26ft 0in to 27ft 0in.

In April 1936, William Bramham obtained a post as Works Manager of the Lowestoft coach factory of Eastern Counties Omnibus Co Ltd. He tendered his resignation at Roe's effective from 9 May 1936 and took up his new position on 18 May 1936. On 1 July 1936, the coach factory was separated from the ECOC Ltd to become Eastern Coach Works Ltd with Bramham in charge as Director and General Manager.

In October 1936, Bramham withdrew his objection to the various outstanding 1935 patent applications being proceeded with, provided that ECW Ltd enjoyed the same rights as Charles H. Roe Ltd.

When Bramham left Roe's in May 1936, the position of Works Manager was filled by Algernon Ewart Webb, who had joined Roe some six months earlier to promote sales. On 1 January 1938, A. E. Webb was appointed to the Roe board at the same time as Bramham sold his shares.

During 1937, the works were further expanded by the construction of a new erecting shop and then in 1938 by the building of a new office block providing a new, impressive frontage to the works. To finance these extensions, a further first mortgage for £15,000 was secured on 31 January 1938.

By the end of 1938, the total floor space at the factory was now 112,000sq ft.

After Mr and Mrs Roe moved into Boston Hall, Boston Spa, Mr Webb, the Works Manager, became the new resident of 'Fairfield', although he still retained 'The Cottage' at Wath, Pateley Bridge.

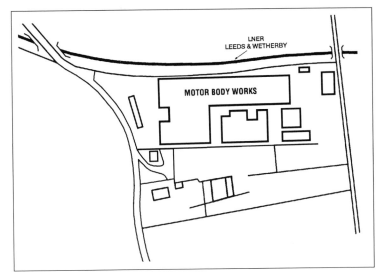

On 1 February 1939, John Isaac Moulton, a solicitor, was elected to the board. At the same time, the tentative enquiries from both English Electric Co Ltd and Metro Cammell Weymann Co Ltd for a merger or outright purchase of Roe were discussed.

On 24 February 1939, the company obtained an independent valuation of £67,075 for its freehold works on the basis of a 'Going Concern'.

The company took over the management of Bintex, manufacturers of foam rubber seat cushions, on 2 November 1939. Bintex was situated in a factory built in 1938 at Pannel near Otley by the maintenance men from Crossgates. Charles H. Roe had been a director of Bintex since it was formed.

With the outbreak of World War 2 in September 1939, the demand from government contracts caused production to be erratic. The financing of these contracts caused a further mortgage of £30,000 to be secured *pari passu* with the two £15,000 ones on 2 May 1940.

The demand for large-capacity passenger-carrying vehicles to operate within many of the Royal Ordnance Factories and other government establishments was met by the Transportation Department of the Ministry of Supply ordering 100 articulated trailer buses comprising a standard Bedford OXC tractor unit with a composite timber and steel Roe body built on a British Trailer or Dyson semi-trailer chassis. The new vehicles were 33ft long and 8ft 5in wide, which allowed three-and-two seating to be arranged either side of the central gangway. Fifty wood-slatted seats were provided together with handrails and hanging straps for a further 15 standees.

These new vehicles, completed between September

1941 and May 1942, were known as 'Bevin' buses after the then Minister of Transport, Mr Ernest Bevin, had inspected the first one. A further two were built for Liverpool Corporation in May 1942 for use between Black Bull and Kirkby. However, these vehicles were only 7ft 6in wide, seated 39 passengers and remained in service until 1944. The only other two articulated trailer buses to operate as public service vehicles were supplied to Mansfield District Traction Co Ltd in May 1942, this time using Commer tractor units and Weymann 40-seat bodies built on British Trailer semi-trailer chassis.

A further 48 articulated trailer chassis were fitted with Roe-built Sleeper or Kitchen bodies.

To meet the demand for public transport in areas involved with war work, in 1942 the Ministry of War Transport allowed restricted manufacture of motor and trolleybuses. Daimler and Guy were allowed to build double-deck chassis whilst Bedford supplied single-deck ones. Roe bodied 240 of the Bedfords and 408 Guy Arab double-deck chassis, 390 of which were fitted with lowbridge type bodies. Nineteen Daimlers with highbridge bodies were also built as well as 64 trolleybus bodies – one on a reconditioned Daimler chassis for South Shields, 10 fitted with lowbridge bodies for St Helens, and the other 53 having normal-height bodies.

On 26 January 1945, John Isaac Moulton, a director of C. H. Roe Ltd, died and his seat on the board was filled by the appointment of John Kennedy Macpherson, a chartered accountant, on 27 January.

On 18 December 1945, the nominal capital of the company was increased from £12,000 to £108,000.

In February 1946, the freehold works were again subject to a revaluation on the basis of a going concern. The valuation concluded that the nett working space was approximately 110,500sq ft and, with the undeveloped part of the site, was valued at £98,000 plus a further £6,000 for 'Fairfield', the cottage and gardens.

By this time, the first bodies to be built to peacetime specifications were leaving the works for Bury Corporation and Leeds City Transport.

On 1 April 1946, William Hamilton Davies, the Assistant Works Manager, was offered the position of Director and General Manager of the Mumford Body & Engineering Co, Lydney, and Mr Davies moved there on 1 May 1946. During the next few months, discussions took place between Mumford and Roe about possible amalgamation of the two companies. In July 1947, Western Motor Holdings sold its interest in Mumford, and by the end of 1947, the Lydney business was renamed Lydney Coach Works. W. H. Davies resigned as Director and General Manager of Lydney on 1 September 1948 and returned to Crossgates as the technical sales representative and was eventually appointed to the Board of Directors in November 1962. Meanwhile, on 21 July 1947, Park Royal Vehicles Ltd acquired a controlling interest in Charles H. Roe Ltd and three existing directors, John Thomas Roe, Hargreaves Brotherton and John Kennedy Macpherson, resigned to be replaced by W. R. Black and Sir Joseph Napier Bart, both Park Royal nominees. The purchase price was agreed at £237,500, and the Park Royal share capital was increased to £875,000 to help finance the purchase. Charles Henry Roe then joined the board of Park Royal Vehicles Ltd.

Above left:
The revolutionary 1935 Show exhibit on the Roe stand was this all-metal-bodied AEC Regent for Leeds City Transport No 200, CNW 901. It had been built to the designs of W. Bramham and incorporated the safety staircase invented by W. Vane Morland, the Leeds manager.

Above and below:
By 1936 the Roe double-deck body had evolved into a handsome shape with a well-rounded single-skin roof. This example No 67, XG 4257, on a Leyland Titan TD4C chassis, is one of three supplied to Middlesbrough Corporation in August 1936 with Roe 56-seat bodies. The upper deck interior depicted is one of the Leyland TTB4 trolleybuses numbered 48-51, supplied in March 1936 to South Lancashire Transport.

Above:
The corresponding design for bodies required on routes with low bridges is typified by Middlesbrough Corporation No 69, XG 4393, one of three Leyland TD4C chassis delivered in November 1936 with 52-seat Roe bodies.

Below:
East Yorkshire Motor Services Ltd was one of many companies which found that rebodying existing motorbus chassis could prolong their life. Roe had rebodied two Leyland Lion PLSC3 buses in 1935 for them, and in 1936 Roe rebodied six 1929 Leyland TS2 chassis and fitted them with 30-seat, rear-entrance bodies to BEF design. No 123, KH 7917, had originally been fitted with a Hall Lewis coach body.

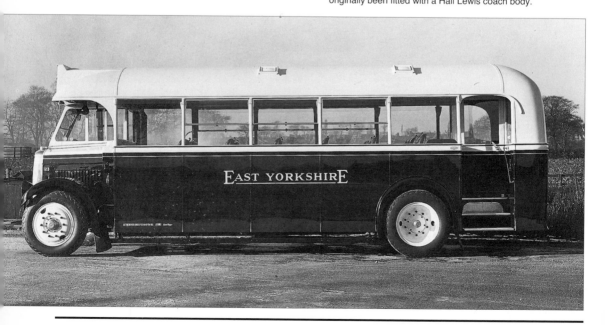

Left and below:
West Hartlepool Corporation was the only customer to purchase Roe centre-entrance double-deck motorbuses with fully enclosed front-engined driving cabs. Four were supplied in March 1937 and a further four followed in April 1938. The 48-seat bodies were mounted on Daimler COG5 chassis. One of the 1937 examples, No 1, EF 6321, is seen on a dull day in March, before despatch from Crossgates.

Below:
Grimsby Corporation continued to purchase centre-entrance
double-deck motorbuses and in July 1937 received a further
six AEC Regents, Nos 58-63, JV 5931-6, which were
despatched from Crossgates. Grimsby was one of the last
operators still to specify petrol-engined chassis.

Right
Kippax & District Motor Co, an independent, operating a
service into Leeds, purchased its first Roe body mounted on an
AEC Regal chassis in July 1937. Fleet No 10, BYG 147 had a
32-seat body. The vehicle was painted in a style which was in
vogue in the late 1930s and was a variation of the ones used
by Lancashire United, West Riding and Yorkshire Traction for
vehicles which were used for seaside express service
duplicates at weekends. Another interesting feature is the little
upright pointer on the front nearside mudguard to assist the
driver to manoeuvre in confined spaces.

Below:
For the 1937 CM Show, the Leeds manager, W. Vane Morland, had designed the 'Leeds City Pullman' which was displayed on the AEC stand. This time the AEC Regent, fleet No 400, FNW 719, had a traditional half-cab-style driver's cab, but the body style had been redesigned so that the lower saloon had four side windows instead of the usual five on Roe bodies, or six on many other bodies from other manufacturers. All the side windows were deeper, giving better visibility for passengers

and driver. The body was constructed to the Roe composite patents using teak for the main body frame which was built on an English oak underframe. The Roe safety staircase, designed in 1935 by W. Vane Morland, was incorporated. The vehicle was also fitted with the Leeds patent emergency brake which had been developed to allow the vehicle to be parked by braking all four wheels. This brake could also be applied by the conductor or passengers in the event of the driver collapsing at the wheel. AEC/courtesy author's collection

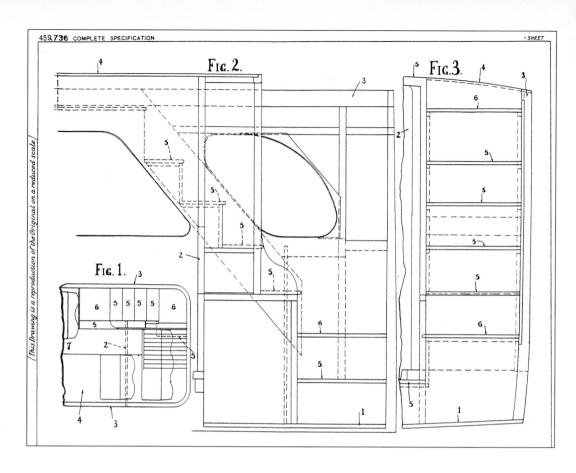

Fig. 2.

Fig. 3.

Fig. 1.

Left:
Patent staircase.

Below left:
An interesting order for a double-deck motorbus body was completed by Crossgates on 30 December 1937. The AEC Regent was fitted with a Roe body incorporating the safety staircase and was very similar to a batch of 30 being supplied at that time to Leeds. In this case, the vehicle was for the West Bromwich Corporation fleet. Numbered 70, EA 9064, it was purchased for comparison purposes before the withdrawal of the Corporation's tram services. Being unsuccessful, no further orders followed.

Below:
Two operators purchased Roe-bodied single-deck motorbuses with enclosed driver's cab. The first was Oldham Corporation which placed three Leyland Tiger TS6 examples into service in 1934 with Roe 32-seat bodies for use on the three express services linking Manchester with Uppermill, New Hey or Greenfield. The other customer was West Hartlepool Corporation which placed two Daimler COG5 single-deck buses with 35-seat Roe bodies into service in April 1938. EF 6726, fleet No 26, was one of the two.

Below:
Northampton Corporation purchased 10 Daimler COG5 chassis with 55-seat double-deck Roe bodies. Fitted with the Roe safety staircase and without the curved side window, they seated 25 in the lower saloon. Numbered 101-5, VV 7873-7 were completed in May 1939 and a further five, 106-10, followed in August 1939. The elaborate lining-out had become outdated by the late 1930s.

Above:
South Shields Corporation was another Daimler COG5 user and in August 1939 took delivery of one fitted with a forward-entrance 56-seat Roe body, numbered 122, CU 4418.

Below:
As World War 2 caused disruption to bus body building, other work was undertaken by Roe, such as converting a Vauxhall 20 car into an emergency ambulance for Leeds Corporation.

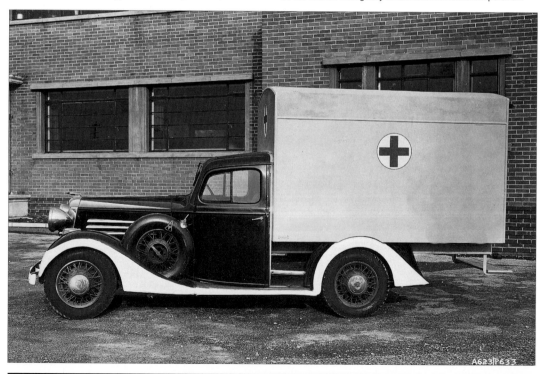

Above:

After war started in September 1939, ECW Ltd at Lowestoft had difficulties in getting materials for body construction. Roe, however, had materials but lacked chassis and when West Riding could not get its Leyland TD7 chassis for 15 lowbridge bodies, the materials in manufacture were used for other orders. It seems likely that the Roe works agreed to body five Bristol K5G chassis using some of the parts from this contract, and United Counties was able to obtain quickly these five vehicles numbered 567-71, BBD 811-15, which were completed in May 1940. At the same time ECW Ltd was forced to close its Lowestoft factory and move to a former United

Counties OC Ltd depot at Irthlingborough for the rest of the war. No 567 is seen outside Crossgates and looks like a normal Roe lowbridge body, with six-bay construction instead of the five normally built by Roe; various ECW features had been incorporated probably to allow standardisation with the existing fleet.

Below:

By June 1940, sufficient Leyland TD7 chassis had been released to allow Roe to complete the five highbridge double-deck buses for Sunderland District Omnibus Co Ltd, fleet Nos 170-4, EPT 693-7.

Above:
In July 1940, Yorkshire Electric Power Co, Thornhill Power Station, Dewsbury, had a Roe workshop body fitted to a Leyland Lynx chassis. HD 7236 was identified by YEP as Leyland No 3.

Below:
Leigh Corporation was able to obtain three Leyland TS11 chassis for which Roe was able to complete the bodies in November and December 1940; fleet numbers were 78-80, ETJ 107-9. This view of No 80 proclaims that the Leigh manager was R. Le Fevre, who later moved to Bury and then Halifax.

Right:
Caledonian Omnibus Co Ltd sent a secondhand Dennis Lancet I chassis to Crossgates for a new body. Roe fitted a body which had been designed to be the 1939 CM Show exhibit in the colours of West Riding on a Leyland TS8 chassis. With the cancellation of the show after the outbreak of war it had not been completed, and so the hybrid vehicle was despatched in March 1941 as Caledonian No 254 EPD 594. Incidentally, the body was intended to be the prototype for a new single-deck body with larger windows.

Below:
Pickfords the heavy haulage specialists purchased a special heavy duty haulage tractor in late 1940 from J. & H. McLaren Ltd, Hunslet, Leeds. Roe, having built the cabs and bodywork for the Leeds steam haulage manufacturers for many years, was the subcontractor for the cab on this unusual machine.

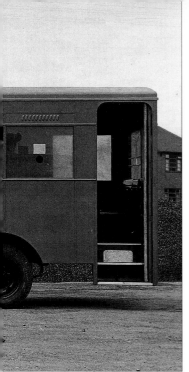

Below:
In January 1942 both Yorkshire Woollen District and Yorkshire Traction were allocated a Leyland Titan TD7 with a Roe highbridge body built to a wartime specification. The YTC one, fleet No 703, HE 9713, was supplied in wartime grey without a fleet name, but the austerity wartime Roe transfer was still applied to the waistrail. The utility specification included the angular rear dome intended to simplify construction.

Above:
The Ministry of Supply Transportation Department placed orders with Roe to build the passenger bodywork of 100 50-seat articulated trailer buses for use inside many of the Royal Ordnance Factories. The tractor unit was a Bedford OXC permanently coupled to a trailer chassis built by either R. A. Dyson and or British Trailer. Roe built the 50-seat bodies which were 8ft 5in wide. After the first one was demonstrated to Mr Ernest Bevin of the Ministry of Transport they were known as 'Bevin Buses'.

Left:
Caledonian Omnibus Co Ltd sent another elderly chassis to Crossgates to have another body fitted. This time it was an AEC Regent which acquired a lowbridge body using West Riding parts. The vehicle, No 239, VX 4902, was completed in January 1942 and the destination blind displayed when photographed is for the Edinburgh to Dumfries service, which was one of the longest routes operated by Caledonian. The body was unusual in having two steps to the rear platform, instead of the usual one. Incidentally, eight Leyland TD7 buses with Roe lowbridge bodies built from stock parts were supplied to West Riding between September 1941 and April 1942.

Right:
During February and March 1942 further Leyland TD7 chassis were bodied by Roe for Crosville Motor Services and Plymouth Corporation. This time the utility specification bodies were lowbridge examples. The first of these, Plymouth Corporation No 27 CDR 354, was completed in February 1942.

Above:
The Ministry of Works 'Flying Squad' order for 12 articulated trailer Kitchen vans, again using Bedford OXC tractor units, was completed in April 1942, and was followed by 48 articulated sleeper trailers which had the same body shells and profile.

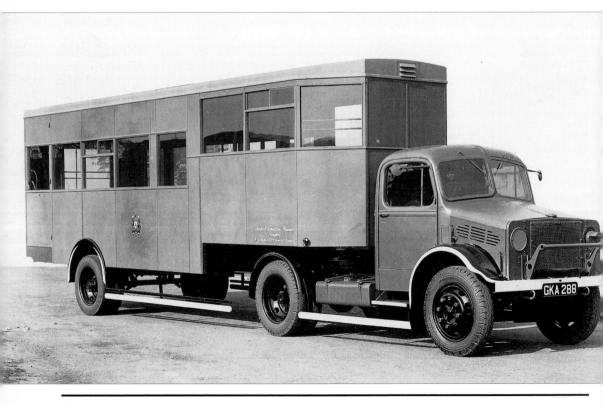

Below left, above and below:
Liverpool Corporation was allocated two articulated trailer buses in May 1942. The Bedfords were registered GKA 287/8 and allocated Nos L873/4 in the Liverpool fleet. The 39-seat Roe bodies were 7ft 6in wide and, like other wartime deliveries, were fitted with wood-slatted seats. The trailer chassis had been manufactured in Liverpool by R. A. Dyson Ltd. Special dispensation had been obtained to allow these to run on public roads and they were only used between Black Bull and Kirkby. In 1944 they were withdrawn from service and converted into canteens in 1945.

Above and right:
In 1942 the Ministry of Supply ordered 240 bodies for fitting to Bedford OWB petrol-engined chassis. They were completed between July 1942 and July 1943 before being allocated by the MoWT to customers and delivered in a brownish livery. The bodies were built to the same drawings by Duple, C. H. Roe and Scottish Motor Traction Co. A further order for another 60 bodies was placed with Roe, but was then transferred to Mulliner to allow Roe to build a large number of double-deck bodies on Daimler and Guy chassis for the MoWT.

Top:
The Ministry of Supply placed two orders for a total of 68 mobile printing press bodies to be mounted on special Foden six-wheel chassis which were 8ft 6in wide. These were completed by Roe between November 1942 and October 1944.

Above:
The need for new trolleybuses during the war was, once the supply of new chassis ceased, initially met by the Ministry of War Transport arranging for ones in seaside resorts such as Bournemouth and Southend to be hired to operators desperate for vehicles. South Shields acquired two former demonstrators, one from Bournemouth and one from Daimler, the latter being rebodied with a new utility style body in September 1942 by Roe. Once the MoWT allowed limited production of new trolleybus chassis in Wolverhampton, 63 of the 468 built had new bodies built by Roe, and of these 10 had lowbridge bodies for St Helens Corporation. One of the first of these MoWT W4 trolleybuses was Teesside No 13, CPY 311, which was completed in December 1944, with a Sunbeam badge.

Above:
When the war ended in 1945 a considerable number of vehicles were still in the process of being manufactured. Roe at Crossgates built its last utility motorbus body, mounted on a Guy Arab chassis, in January 1946 and its last utility trolleybus body in May 1946. As material supplies improved, the supply of new vehicles to peacetime standards resumed and in February 1946 the first of the 15 Leyland PD1 double-deck motorbuses for Bury Corporation fleet, Nos 102-16 EN 8536-50, left Crossgates. The body retained the five-bay construction, incorporated the Roe safety staircase, and seated 56 with 31 in the upper saloon. In 1946 114 bodies were built with this type of staircase.

Right:
Oldham Corporation had placed orders for new buses with Leyland Motors Ltd and C. H. Roe in 1942, but unable to get permits for these, had to wait until the war was over to abandon its final tram routes. The 14 Leyland PD1 double-deck buses delivered in 1946 to Oldham were 7ft 6in wide, numbered 228-241, DBU 20-33. These were followed in 1947 by 50 Leyland PD1/3 chassis with the first Roe-built 8ft 0in-wide bodies for use on routes which had been approved by the North West Traffic Commissioners. This view of 235, one of the 7ft 6in-wide examples, shows the arrangement of the staircase which extended into the lower saloon on the offside reducing the seating capacity. The offside rear saloon bulkhead was repositioned to allow more space for luggage under the steps. The used ticket box and discharge flap for the cleaners to empty it is a reminder that used syringes were not discarded in those days.

Above:
The first new AEC buses to be bodied by Roe after the war were the 20 AEC Regent III RT type models which, due to bodybuilders not being ready to body them for London, were passed to Roe for provincial users. These were completed in November and December 1946 for three operators, West Riding receiving nine with centre-entrance bodies. Grimsby Corporation had three and the other eight were supplied to Halifax – four for the Corporation 'A' fleet and four for the JOC 'B' fleet. No 210, one of the 'B' fleet examples, registered JX 9406, was completed in November 1946 and was placed into service on the joint route to Huddersfield, where the two joint committees faced competition from Huddersfield

Corporation trolleybuses between Huddersfield and Elland. Prior to the war this meant using special buses and Halifax JOC used four 9.6-litre twin carburettor petrol-engined AEC Regents with Roe bodies to compete with the trolleybuses. The new Regent III buses, however, were still left standing by the 70-seat trolleybuses despite the fact that the buses had fewer stops per mile.

Below:
J. Bullock & Sons (1928) Ltd – B&S Motor Services – was one of a number of operators needing lowbridge buses for its services in the West Riding. In April 1947 it received six AEC Regent III motorbuses with 53-seat Roe bodies.

8. Changes in Ownership, 1947-84

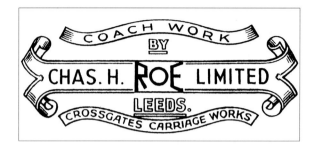

After Park Royal Vehicles Ltd had purchased all the share capital of Charles H. Roe Ltd in July 1947, the first sign of changes in the company was the substitution of a Park Royal metal-framed body for the last of the 20 Roe composite bodies ordered by Leeds City Transport in 1947. This entered service in Leeds in June 1949.

During 1949 the company built a repair shop on the undeveloped land after receiving an enquiry from Plymouth Corporation for reconditioning 100 Guys.

In April 1949 Park Royal Vehicles Ltd was purchased by Associated Commercial Vehicles Ltd, which already owned AEC, Crossley and Maudsley. When Northern Coach Builders at Newcastle went out of business in January 1951, Crossgates bought machinery and timber from the receiver.

In March 1951 the company considered taking over the work in progress at Lincs Trailer Co, Scunthorpe, which was building half-deck coaches to the design of Crellin-Duplex patents, one example being inspected at Crossgates by the ACV Board. In the event, ACV did not take up this option and in late 1951, Mann Egerton & Co Ltd, Norwich, acquired the patents and built a number of examples.

Algernon Ewart Webb resigned on 25 March 1952 and was replaced by James Edward Pearson, who became a director, and General Manager. Charles Henry Roe resigned from his Managing Director position with effect from 30 June 1952 but continued to be the company's Chairman.

After 1951 Park Royal stopped building composite double-deck bodies and passed these over to Roe at Crossgates. Other Park Royal orders began to be subcontracted to Roe, thus from 1953 some of the bodies were finished by Roe or were built at Crossgates using PRV frames or bodyshells.

Once the demand for new service buses started falling in 1950, Roe was able to build a small number of coach bodies. Ten built in 1951 for Lancashire United and six in 1952 for West Riding were built on 30ft chassis with traditional half cabs. Lancashire United purchased six underfloor-engined coach bodies in 1952, whilst East Yorkshire took delivery of 16 double-deck coach-bodied Leyland Titans for use on its express services to and from the east coast.

In September 1953 Roe decided to market 12 new coach bodies called the Dalesman I which were built on AEC Reliance chassis. Further batches of Mark II, III, and IV Dalesman coaches were built in the following years and the last one was completed in July 1959.

When ACV closed the Stockport works of Crossley Motors in 1957 some of the equipment was purchased by Roe for use at Crossgates.

On 24 March 1958 both Sir Joseph Napier Bart and Edward Warwick Broadbent resigned from the board and on 22 November 1958 Rowland Stanley Boshell became a director and Assistant General Manager.

The introduction in 1959 of rear-engined double-deck buses on Leyland Atlantean chassis meant that demand from various BET companies for bodies was satisfied by Park Royal designing all-metal bodies which were then manufactured by Roe.

A high capacity double-deck bus with a forward-entrance body was developed in conjunction with Guy Motors Ltd and the West Riding Automobile Co Ltd at Wakefield. Roe built bodies for 131 out of the 137 Guy

Double-deck bodies fitted with Roe patent staircase. Patent No 459.763	
Year	No delivered
1935	1
1936	42
1937	68
1938	60
1939	64
1940	17
1941	4
1942	0
1943	0
1944	0
1945	0
1946	114
1947	72
1948	85
1949	91
1950	159
Total	**777**

Summary of bodies built at Crossgates by Roe 1928-84. (A period where reasonable records exist.)

	Double-deck		Single-	Trailer	Trolleybuses		Other bodies	Total
	Normal height	Low bridge	deck	buses	Double- deck	Single- deck		
1928	7		48		10	4	2	71
1929	1	1	74		7		4	87
1930	13		72		18			103
1931	24		44		27	3	1	99
1932	108		37					145
1933	29	2	48		17			96
1934	80		81					161
1935	82		58		7		1	148
1936	63	14	137		17			231
1937	99	12	135		3			249
1938	100	16	102		43			261
1939	87	16	78		23	3		207
1940	17	9	29		5		26	86
1941	7	8	1	70	4		42	132
1942	10	42	106	32	2		52	244
1943	17	81	135				29	262
1944	22	148			4		36	210
1945		125			40			165
1946	134	17	10		20			181
1947	135	8	59		13			215
1948	119	14	66		29			228
1949	149	27	76		10			262
1950	197	37	16		8			258
1951	80	5	22		22			129
1952	106	7	64		5			182
1953	132	4	21		11		2 trams	170
1954	108	15	44		15			182
1955	101	23	28		14		4 vans	170
1956	152	21	42		14		2 vans	231
1957	184	50	17		12			263
1958	145	5	24		21		10 pick-ups	205
1959	143	2	30		20			195
1960	135	3	13		23		3 pick-ups	177
1961	138		31		10			179
1962	177		20		10			207
1963	187		13		2			202
1964	164		11		2			177
1965	162		24					186
1966	136		8					144
1967	107		54					161
1968	113		43					156
1969	143		8					151
1970	144		12					156
1971	121		20					141
1972	117		23					140
1973	151							151
1974	108							108
1975	131							131
1976	136							136
1977	132							132
1978	135							135
1979	142							142
1980	181						1 artic s-d	182
1981	147						6 artic s-ds	153
1982	120							120
1983	84		10				13 underframes	107
1984	86		22					108
Total								**9,610**

Average number of bodies per year = 168

Total no of bodies built at Crossgates in excess of 10,000

Wulfrunian chassis built between November 1959 and March 1965. The revolutionary design allowed a low-height double-deck bus to be built with centre gang-ways in both saloons.

In June 1962 the ACV group merged with the Leyland group to become the Leyland Motor Corporation. Shortly after the merger Charles Henry Roe resigned on 30 September 1962 from his position as Chairman of Charles H. Roe Ltd. He was now 75 years old and died three years later on 30 November 1965. On 22 November 1962, William Rushton Black resigned from the board, while Walter Edward Dodsworth and William Hamilton Davies joined it.

In 1965, the Transport Holding Co acquired a 30%

holding of the share capital of Park Royal Vehicles Ltd. In 1968 the British Motor Corporation and the Leyland Motor Corporation merged to form the British Leyland Motor Corporation.

While production of bodies continued at both the Park Royal and Roe factories, the industry was starting to contract. Daimler and Guy were the first casualties, followed by AEC in 1979 and then, in 1981, Park Royal closed, leaving Roe as the sole survivor of the ACV group. With pressure to move production to the Workington factory with the rationalisation of its product range, and since its remaining factories were all short of work, BLMC decided to close Crossgates in September 1984.

Above:
In 1939 West Riding Automobile Co Ltd placed orders for 60 new double-deck Roe bodies to be fitted to Leyland TD7 chassis. Forty-five were for the 'red' ex-tramway fleet with centre-entrance bodies and the other 15 were to be lowbridge buses for the green fleet. Roe records suggest that this order was considered complete after delivering 52 lowbridge bodies, eight on Leyland TD7 chassis and 44 on Guy Arab chassis, with seven of the Guys being painted red. It also seems that the nine AEC RT type Regent III chassis supplied in 1946 may have been allocated by the MoWT to complete this order. In the event, in 1948 and 1949, the red fleet received 53 new AEC Regent III double-deck buses with Roe centre-entrance 50-seat bodies, numbered 65-117. No 117 was the last centre-entrance bus to be built by Roe in July 1949. This view of No

67 shows the new type waistrail introduced in 1945 where a flat strip of steel was rolled to shape with the edges doubled over and folded at right angles to add strength. The upper deck waistrail was similar but a smaller section. This was given patent No 619,494.

Right:
Blair & Palmer Ltd, in 1946, was the first company in Carlisle to place postwar buses into service. The two highbridge double-deck buses had Roe bodies mounted on Daimler CD chassis. In June 1948 two similar buses joined them, this time being fitted with high-backed seats and platform doors, again a first for the district. They were used on the 15-mile contract service to the Royal Naval Air Station at Anthorn for staff and personnel.

Above:
Oldham Corporation ordered 10 Leyland PS1 chassis with Roe 32-seat front-entrance bodies. Unable to get the chassis from Leyland, Oldham found it necessary to purchase Crossley 7ft 6in-wide SD42/3 chassis instead. Numbered 292-301, DBU 292-301, they were completed and despatched to Oldham in February 1948. A further four 7ft 6in-wide Roe bodies were supplied in February 1950 on Crossley SD42/7 chassis numbered 362-5.

Above and below:
Leeds City Transport continued the prewar tradition of displaying a vehicle at the 1948 CM Show; this time the exhibit was another 'Leeds City Pullman' Roe body on an AEC Regent III chassis, 8ft wide, numbered 600, MNW 600. At the same time the first 25 Roe-bodied Leeds City Pullmans were ordered, again on AEC Regent III 7ft 6in-wide chassis, which entered service from August 1949. These were the first production Pullmans and were numbered 451-75, MUG 451-75.

Above:
Initially after the war Roe was able to persuade the BET companies that it would be quicker and cheaper to supply standard bodies rather than build examples to the Federation design. However, County Motors (Lepton) Ltd, Huddersfield, a company jointly owned by West Riding, Yorkshire Traction and Yorkshire Woollen (one independent and two BET companies) placed an order for 10 BET-style 32-seat single-deck bodies. Delivery of the first six, Nos 73-8, commenced in December 1948 on Leyland PS1 chassis, and the last four, Nos 83-86, were delivered in late 1949 on Leyland PS2 chassis.

Below:
Bradford Corporation, having been allocated a number of 8ft-wide trolleybuses diverted from an overseas order by the MoWT, was able to get consent to operate further 8ft examples on the cross-city route from Crossflats to Bradford Moor, so 12 BUT type 9611T trolleybuses were delivered in late 1948 and early 1949, numbered 740-51, EKU 740-51. In 1950 the Ministry of Transport consented to the general introduction of 8ft-wide vehicles, and single-deck vehicles up to 30ft long.

Above:
Leeds City Transport ordered 20 AEC Regent III chassis with 7ft 6in Roe bodies in 1947. Park Royal Vehicles Ltd had just acquired all the shares of Charles H. Roe Ltd and much thought was given to rationalisation between the two companies. The first 19 entered service between July and December 1948 with five-bay Roe bodies. The last chassis however was fitted with a Park Royal metal-framed four-bay body built to meet the requirements of the Leeds manager W. Vane Morland to allow comparison with the Roe composite bodies. This one was not finished by Roe until June 1949. It was numbered 450, LUA 450, and was placed in service just before the first of the 'Leeds City Pullmans'. But with Morland retiring Leeds was not to be moved and continued to support traditional composite bodies for many more years although metal-framed ones were purchased from MCW.

Below:
Transport Vehicles (Daimler) Ltd selected Roe to build the body for a demonstration motorbus intended for the South African market. The Daimler CD650 chassis fitted with a 56-seat Roe body 8ft wide was completed in May 1949.

Top:
The last Roe bodies to be supplied to J. Bullock & Sons (1928) Ltd, owners of the B&S Motor Service, were delivered in September 1949 with 32-seat front-entrance bodies 7ft 6in wide built on two Guy Arab III chassis with Meadows engines. In September 1950 the B&S business was purchased for about £500,000 by the West Riding Automobile Co Ltd.

Above:
While the B&S body looked fussy, the bodies on 10 Leyland PS2 single-deck buses for Lancashire United had a clean outline. The 30-seat Roe bodies were fitted with semi-coach seats for use on the various long-distance routes operated jointly with other companies such as the Liverpool-Newcastle service. Numbered 395-404, KTJ 301-10, they entered service in September 1949.

Above:

Many operators lacked materials and resources to maintain buses properly and after the war, faced with expensive repairs when the current certificate of fitness expired, found that it was more economical to fit a new body after refurbishing the chassis. Among the Tilling Group companies to purchase new Roe bodies for reconditioned chassis were Lincolnshire Road Car, United Automobile Services and West Yorkshire Road Car. In early 1950 20 prewar Bristol K5G chassis from the United and West Yorkshire companies were fitted with new Roe 55-seat lowbridge bodies. No K366, BWY 998, was one of six allocated to the Keighley-West Yorkshire Joint Services Ltd fleet.

Below:

E. Hartness, based in Penrith, was another operator to order new bodies for reconditioned Daimler CVD6 chassis, this time specifying Roe 56-seat highbridge bodies with high-backed seats and platform doors which were completed in May 1950.

Above:
In 1948, St Helens Corporation, having placed orders with East Lancashire Coachbuilders in July 1946 for eight single-deck bodies on Bristol L6A chassis, had to find another supplier after East Lancs asked to be released from the contract. Roe agreed to build them in September 1948. In 1949 three similar bodies were built on reconditioned Leyland TS6 chassis and then in July 1950 Roe completed a further three bodies mounted on reconditioned Leyland TS7 chassis. This time, however, Roe fitted 33-seat dual-door Pullman-style bodies with deeper windows. St Helens 253 was one of the last three. Unusually, all 14 had no canopy over the bonnet and were thus similar to other East Lancs bodies supplied to Rotherham and others.

Below:
In 1950 Huddersfield Corporation refurbished seven prewar Karrier E6 trolleybus chassis and arranged for Roe to supply seven body shells which were completed and trimmed by the corporation using seat frames and fittings salvaged from the original bodies. In August 1950, three months after the bodyshell left Crossgates, the first one, No 493, entered service. After this, further rebodied trolleybuses were completely finished by the bodybuilder before delivery. At the same time 14 new Sunbeam MS2 trolleybuses were supplied with 70-seat Roe bodies, numbered 593-606. The first one, No 593, was displayed at the 1950 CM Show.

Right:
Another exhibit at the 1950 CM Show was an AEC Regal IV fitted with 40 dual-purpose seats. This was the first body to be built by Roe on one of the new underfloor chassis, which, since the alteration in Public Service Vehicle legislation, could now be 8ft wide and 30ft long. The body was constructed on a metal framework and was painted in the colours of the West Riding Automobile Co with fleet No 706, registration DHL 166. The front-entrance doorway was very narrow and did not find favour with West Riding, which did not place this vehicle into service after the show. Instead, Roe built a further example with a centre-entrance body, still seating 40. This entered service in July 1951 as fleet No 709, DHL 686.

Left:
Ramsbottom UDC was the first operator to place three Roe 44-seat buses into service to the new maximum dimensions. These Leyland 'Royal Tiger' buses entered service in November 1950, fleet Nos 26-8, MTC 255-7. They had wider doors and less overhang at the rear than the show exhibit.

Right:
In March 1951, one of the half-decker coaches built by the Lincs Trailer Co of Scunthorpe to the Crellin-Duplex patents was examined at Crossgates by officials of the ACV Group with a view to Roe taking over the work in progress at Lincs Trailer. This idea did not proceed, possibly due to the introduction by the group of the AEC Regal IV underfloor chassis. In September 1951 Mann Egerton & Co Ltd of Norwich acquired the rights and produced a number on both underfloor- and forward-engined chassis.

Top:
In 1952 two companies in the Coast Lines Group, Belfast Steamship Co and David MacBrayne Ltd placed orders with ACV for a number of new buses. Previously AEC and Maudsley chassis with Park Royal bodywork had been favoured since 1929 by both companies. This time AEC supplied four Regal III and two Regal IV chassis, with Roe building four 27ft 6in-long and 7ft 6in-wide bodies on the Regal IIIs with 35-seat front entrances. The two Regal IVs had 44-seat Roe bodies 30ft by 8ft. MLV 683 was supplied in February 1952 to Liverpool for use on the connecting service between Princes Landing Stage and the three mainline stations. In December 1952 the other five were dispatched to MacBrayne's.

Above:
Darlington Corporation purchased 22 Guy Arab single-deck motorbuses 30ft long and 8ft wide to replace many of its single-deck trolleybuses. Fourteen were delivered in early 1952 and a further eight in late 1953. Like the trolleybuses they replaced, the Roe bodies, seating 41, had centre entrances.

Top:
In the period following World War 2, United Automobile Services Ltd was one of the major operators which separated bodies from chassis when carrying out major recertification work when the initial seven-year certificate of fitness expired. The bus could only be issued with a new certificate of fitness after a certifying officer had carried out a detailed examination. While a new body had usually a seven-year certificate of fitness, it was more usual for the next one to be for five years or less if the body had not been thoroughly overhauled. UAS Ltd in 1949 transferred 14 bodies from prewar vehicles to new Bristol L5G chassis. The first 12 were rebuilt by Woodhall-Nicholson at Halifax and obtained CoFs for five years. In 1951

they were renumbered BG1-12. These 12 were the last bodies to be dealt with by Woodhall-Nicholson. The other two bodies were discarded and instead new Roe 35-seat front-entrance bodies were fitted in 1952, the vehicles becoming BG13 and 14. They survived until 1961 while BG1-12 had to be rebodied again in 1954.

Above:
The first coach bodies to be built by Roe mounted on underfloor chassis were supplied in April 1952 to Lancashire United Transport Ltd. Mounted on Guy Arab UF chassis, the centre-entrance bodies seated 39.

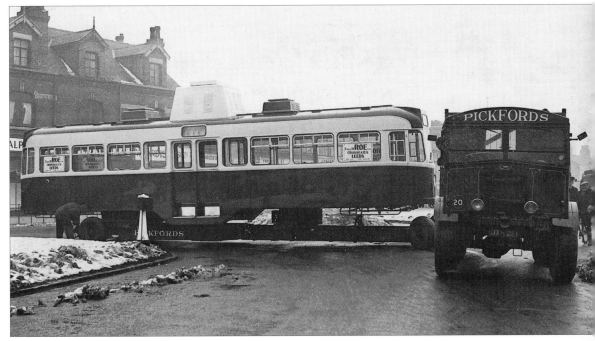

Top:
At the 1952 Commercial Motor Show, G. H. Pulfrey, the enterprising General Manager at Hull, displayed a revolutionary trolleybus for Britain. A 54-seat forward-entrance/centre-exit Roe body had been built on a Sunbeam MF2B chassis and it was Pulfrey's intention that eventually the corporation would use it for one-man operation. As a result, it was fitted with trolley retrievers. In 1954-5 a further 15 were built and they were known as the 'Coronation' type. No 101 is seen before the vehicle left Crossgates for the show.

Above:
In 1952 Leeds City Transport placed orders with Roe to build two single-deck tramcar bodies to the design of the Leeds Manager, Mr A. B. Findlay. The bodies were built on steel underframes fabricated by Patchett & Co Ltd of Leeds. The Roe-patented teak and steel reinforced construction was used throughout. The two saloons on each side of the centre entrance and exits each seated 17 and accommodation was provided for 36 standee passengers in the gangways of the saloons and centre entrance. Delivery caused a number of problems to the contractors in trying to avoid street furniture with the two bodies when delivering them to Leeds from the works. The two trams were numbered 601-2.

Above:
The first order known to have been subcontracted to Roe from Park Royal was the supply of 10 Leyland PD2/12s to Walsall Corporation in 1953, numbered 811-20, RDH 501-10. The 27ft by 8ft double-deck buses were completed in May/June 1953, and like the East Yorkshire double-deck coaches had fully enclosed cabs.

Below:
In September 1953 an experimental lightweight all-metal body was built on an AEC X1594/1 chassis by Park Royal. This vehicle was sent to Roe to be finished. It is very similar to the first Reliance and may well be the same vehicle 50 AMC, new in 1953.

Top and above:
As the original certificate of fitness expired from 1950 onwards, many of the owners of utility-bodied buses refurbished the chassis and purchased new bodies for them. Typical of the 140-plus Guy Arabs rebodied by Roe was Sunderland District

Omnibus Co No 177, one of four (numbered 175-8) rebodied in March 1953. While Sunderland District was a highbridge example, East Midland Motor Services Ltd No D28, GNN 328, was a lowbridge example with a 55-seat Roe body built to a length of 26ft 9in.

Above:
Many operators satisfied with previous deliveries from Crossgates continued to support Roe. One of these was Wolverhampton Corporation which placed seven 7ft 6in-wide Guy Arab IV, 56-seat buses into service in 1953. No 575 was one of the batch numbered 571-7.

Top right and right:
Northampton Corporation ordered 10 new bodies for Daimler CVG6 chassis due for delivery in 1953. The first five, delivered in July, were fitted with five-bay Roe composite bodies with Roe safety staircases and were numbered 190-4, DNH 190-4. The other five, 195-9, delivered in November, were fitted with Roe four-bay all-metal bodies, using one complete shell and four sets of frames from Park Royal. These were similar in appearance to the London RT and both batches were 8ft wide.

Above:
In early 1954 the Coast Lines Group ordered a further three AEC buses for its Liverpool-stations to Princes Landing Stage service to connect with the Irish cross-Channel vessels. This time the Regal III chassis were fitted with 30ft by 8ft 39-seat front-entrance Roe bodies, registered PKD 588-90. They were very similar to the 7ft 6in examples supplied in April 1953 to Doncaster Corporation.

Below:
A separate building was constructed at Crossgates in 1949 to develop the repair side of the business. One of the first major contracts was the lengthening to 29ft 3in of 445 single-deck buses: types S6, S8 and S10 built by the Birmingham Midland Motor Omnibus Co Ltd – Midland Red. These had been built between 1946 and 1950 to the original maximum length of 27ft 6in. Other work done in the repair department was the complete refurbishment of vehicles for customers. Typical of these were six Guy Arab Utility double-deck buses refurbished for Burton-on-Trent Corporation in 1953. No 69, HGC 125, was originally built for London Transport in 1945 and was purchased by Burton from one of the Leeds dealers. In Burton the general view was that the refurbishment cost more than the buses were worth!

Right:
Sunderland Corporation purchased 20 all-metal double-deck bus bodies 27ft 6in long by 7ft 6in wide from Roe in late 1953-4, mounted on Daimler CVG5 chassis. Park Royal supplied Roe with 10 sets of PRV framing and 10 body shells. The 58-seat bodies, numbered 148-67, DBR 648-67, were built to Sunderland's requirement of a maximum body weight of 55cwt.

Below:
West Wales Motors Ltd, Tycroes, Ammanford purchased a Guy Arab UF which was bodied by Roe with a 44-seat front-entrance body. It was numbered 35, JTH 260, and was dispatched in January 1954 to South Wales.

Top:
H. W. Hunter, Seaton Delaval, Northumberland, arranged for
Roe to fit a new body to another reconditioned 1937 Leyland
TS7 chassis. The 39-seat centre-entrance body was built
7ft 10in wide and 28ft 4in long as shown in this works view of
No 21 JR 6600, completed in March 1954, where the body
overhangs the 7ft 6in axles.

Above:
E. Hartness at Penrith had a further four Daimler reconditioned
chassis rebodied in 1954, this time with Roe 35-seat front-
entrance bodies 7ft 6in wide with full-fronted bodywork. GAO
953 was one of two delivered in March, the other two following
in May.

Above:
Llandudno UDC, having introduced a stage carriage service up the Great Orme to St Tudno's Church in 1951, found that the 35-seat Fodens were too large for the traffic in winter, so two Guy Otter 25-seat buses with front-entrance Roe bodies were purchased. Delivered in July 1954, they were used during the summer on the seasonal circular tours around the Marine Drive, which encircles the Great Orme, and in winter they were used on the stage carriage service. The two were registered CCC 596-7.

Right:
Oldham Corporation, in late 1953, ordered 10 Leyland PD2/20 buses with Roe bodies. Delivered between August and October 1954, the buses had Pullman-style bodies fitted to the 'new look' type Leyland chassis.

Above:
ACV Sales Ltd displayed a 41-seat Roe Dalesman II coach-bodied AEC Reliance at the 1954 CM Show. Registered TUG 20, it was demonstrated to a number of operators after the show. Dalesman bodies were built by Roe to fill production gaps in the works, and were usually built for stock, to allow a quick sale once enquiries were received.

Below:
Another operator to place 10 'new look' Leyland PD2/22 double-deck buses into service in 1954 was West Riding Automobile Co Ltd, which continued to purchase 50-seat lowbridge buses for the 'green' fleet. The upper decks accommodated 24 passengers while the double-step entrance to the platform allowed a flat floor into the lower saloon.

Right:
Yorkshire Traction Co Ltd found that the larger 44-seat underfloor single-deck buses were more useful than the earlier 32-seat examples. A number of surplus Leyland PS1 single-deck bus chassis were overhauled and rebodied with Park Royal-style all-metal bodies, 27ft by 7ft 6in, built at Crossgates by Roe with 61 seats. No 1041H, HHE 322, was one of six supplied in February/March 1955, the 'H' signifying a highbridge body. The Yorkshire Traction badge on the radiator and a 'Y' suffix to the original chassis number qualified them for a new Barnsley registration number.

Right:
County Motors (Lepton) Ltd had two 1948 former Roe-bodied Leyland PS1 buses, Nos 75 and 78, rebuilt as 55-seat lowbridge buses in April 1956. Like the Yorkshire Traction examples the bodies were all-metal built by Roe to the Park Royal design. The chassis had been refurbished by Yorkshire Woollen with the chassis number being given a 'WD' suffix. Although finished and painted in County livery with new fleet Nos 91 and 92, Huddersfield Motor Tax refused to issue new registration numbers to a 1948 chassis. Crossgates had to repaint them into Yorkshire Traction livery with fleet Nos 1071 and 1072 so that Barnsley Motor Tax could issue new registration numbers, KHE 649-50. County Motors was given two utility YTC Guys in exchange, which were then renumbered 75 and 78 in the County fleet.

Top:
Cleethorpes Corporation Daimler Freeline No 29, MFU 678, was delivered in June 1955. Its PRV-style body was built by Roe and seated 43.

Above:
When South Lancashire Transport Co started abandoning its trolleybus system in the mid-1950s, many of the replacement Lancashire United vehicles carried South Lancashire Transport Co legal ownership lettering. One such vehicle was Atkinson Alpha PL745H, No 554, one of 10 numbered 552-61, WTB 61-70. It was delivered in late 1955 with a Roe 40-seat body. While having the same bodyshell as the Cleethorpes vehicle the frontal treatment was different.

Above:
One order which did not originate with the PRV group was the supply of four box van bodies on Bedford goods chassis for the Bradford Dyers Association Ltd. The last one to be completed in October 1955 was fleet No 142, MAK 380.

Below:
Another direct order was from W. B. Allen for a mobile X-ray unit comprising a van body built on a Dodge chassis, registered 100 HMD, and a caravan built on a Tasker Trailer. The unit was operated by Portable X-rays Ltd, Chiswick, London.

Top:
When Hartlepool Corporation and West Hartlepool Corporation had a disagreement about the joint service linking the two towns in the 1950s, where previously WHC had operated it on behalf of both corporations, Hartlepool Corporation purchased its first four new motorbuses. The 63-seat Roe bodies were mounted on AEC Regent V chassis and were numbered 1-4, TUP 856-9. They were delivered in April 1956.

Above:
Booth & Fisher operated a number of local services in Killamarsh, and in 1956 placed two new AEC Reliance MU3RV single-deck buses with dual purpose 41-seat Roe bodies into service. Registered 352 and 353 BNU, the destination blind on 352 BNU shows that it is a one-person-operated vehicle – 'Enter and Pay' being more correct than 'Pay and Enter' usually found on OMO vehicles.

Top:
A number of pick-up bodies were fitted to Ford Thames Trader 530E goods chassis for the Uganda Police Force. Ten were supplied during 1958 and a further three followed in 1960. Where Roe placed its transfer is not known.

Above:
The Dalesman IV coach body was introduced at the 1958 CM Show on a Maudslay Reliance chassis. The 43-seat coach was in the colours of Liss & District and was registered UHO 2 in October 1958. How long the 'badge engineering' exhibit retained its Maudslay badge after the show is not known, but it allowed the ACV group additional space at the CM Show.

Left:
Lincoln Corporation purchased seven Leyland Tiger Cubs fitted with all-metal Roe dual-door bodies seating 41, numbered 81-7, MFE 993-9. They were delivered in late 1958.

Right:
The production version of the Dalesman IV coach had a slightly different appearance by the time Black & White Motorways Ltd, Cheltenham Spa order for five AEC Reliances with 41-seat front-entrance Dalesman IVs (numbered 204-8, WDG 630-4) was delivered in early 1959. No 208 is seen outside the Roe offices in March 1959.

Left:
In June 1958 the repair department at Crossgates completed the rebuilding of the first of 12 Park Royal Dennis Lancet J3 single-deck buses. The work involved moving the entrance from rear to front, removing most of the bulkhead and fitting a new fully enclosed front end assembly, so that the vehicle was suitable for one-man operation. The vehicle was dispatched to East Kent Road Car Co Ltd workshops for painting and installation of OMO equipment. Published articles in 1959 suggested that the order had been placed with ACV for 25 vehicles to be rebuilt by Park Royal, and it was later thought that some had been converted in Leeds by Roe. Where the last 13 were converted is not clear.

Above and below:
Liss & District Omnibus Co Ltd operated a stage carriage service from Petersfield to Longmoor. In early 1959 they purchased a 1946 AEC Regent III experimental chassis, No 9612A2611, and had a Roe 56-seat front-entrance lowbridge body fitted to it. The vehicle predated many present day vehicles by having marker lights on the front and rear ends of the roof. It was registered VHO 123. In late 1960 a further AEC Regent III experimental chassis, No U128389, was fitted with an identical front-entrance body incorporating a full-fronted cab and was registered 150 AOU. This was the last side-gangway lowbridge bus body to be built by Roe.

Above:
South Wales Transport Co operated a number of services which went under a very low railway bridge between the docks and Llanelli town centre. The existing half-cab single-deck buses were reaching the end of their lives and the only suitable chassis capable of negotiating the bridge was an AEC Regent V fitted with a restricted height body. Roe built the first two replacements in June 1959 and the body shape resembled the bottom half of a double-deck front-entrance vehicle. No 34, TCY 102, the second vehicle to be built, is seen at the works.

Below:
Barrow Corporation modernised part of its fleet in 1959 when 10 existing Leyland PD2/3 buses, numbered 141-150, had the existing Park Royal bodies removed and broken up. The refurbished chassis were sent to Leeds for Roe to fit new five-bay bodies, seating 59. The last two to be completed, numbered 147 and 148, were fitted with platform doors for use on the route to Ulverston via the Coast Road. The vehicles were dispatched unpainted to Barrow between July 1959 and January 1960 for Barrow Corporation to complete.

Above and below:

Changes in PSV legislation in June 1956 allowed two-axle double-deck buses to be built up to a maximum length of 30ft, although many operators were still content to purchase 27ft-long ones. The traditional composite-framed double-deck body was available in various permutations and these two examples show similar AEC Regent V chassis 30ft long. One customer, Sheffield Joint Omnibus Committee-the 'B' fleet, was purchasing 69-seat Roe-bodied double-deck buses and No 1381, 6331 WJ, was one of 25 supplied in late 1959. 3568 DT was supplied to the Blue Ensign fleet of G. H. Ennifer, one of the Doncaster independents, and in this case a 73-seat front-entrance body was fitted, having shallower lower saloon windows.

Above:
When Leyland Motors Ltd introduced the rear-engined
Atlantean double-deck bus chassis in 1959, Park Royal
designed a 78-seat front-entrance metal-framed body which
was initially built by Roe at Leeds. One of the first examples
was Trent Motor Services Ltd fleet No 1082 RRC 88, one of a
batch of 23 which were numbered 1067-89 and completed in
early 1960. These were followed by others for Devon General,
Northern General and its subsidiaries Tynemouth & District,
Sunderland District and Gateshead & District. Over 80 were
built for these BET companies by September 1960.

Below:
Many of the small independent companies purchased dual-
purpose single-deck buses suitable for stage carriage or
private hire purposes. Felix Motors Ltd, one of the Doncaster
independents, purchased one with a 43-seat Roe body
mounted on an AEC Reliance chassis. Numbered 41,
9629 WU, it was new in April 1960.

Above:
West Riding Automobile Co Ltd operated many routes which needed lowbridge buses. While the Tilling group had developed the Bristol Lodekka, this was not available to other operators which had a limited choice of suitable alternatives. When Guy Motors Ltd came up with a design using a set-back front axle, a forward engine and a dropped centre rear axle it was possible to have a large capacity double-deck bus with conventional centre gangways in both saloons. West Riding became involved with the design after promising to purchase 100 or more. Guy Motors added air suspension and disc brakes to the specification and, in conjunction with Roe, a body with a carrying capacity of up to 78 was designed to pass under bridges with a 13ft 6in headroom. The first Guy

'Wulfrunian' chassis was bodied by Roe and was painted in the West Riding 'red' livery for use on the former tram routes. Numbered 863, OHL 863 was photographed at Nostell Priory, Wakefield in November 1959, prior to being displayed at the Scottish Motor Show.

Below:
7800 DA was one of two Guy Wulfrunian demonstration buses completed in early 1960. Of the 137 Guy Wulfrunians built, Roe bodied 131. The vehicle was not as successful as it should have been due to excessive wear on the disc brakes and failures of the revolutionary suspension, and of the 130 which were operated by West Riding the last one was withdrawn in March 1972.

Top:
Leeds City Welfare Services was another user of a double-deck AEC Regent V chassis fitted with a single-deck body. In this case, Roe built a 27ft by 7ft 6in body with 20 seats and wheelchair access through the doors at the rear of the body. 8895 UB was new in May 1960. A similar vehicle was built in July 1960 for the Coal Industry Social Welfare Organisation; in their case 2690 UG had a body 8ft wide and seated 31.

Above:
The small Huddersfield-based independent, Hansons Buses Ltd, modernised its fleet by having its early postwar AEC Regents and Regals rebuilt before Roe fitted the new body. Seven were rebuilt with 65-seat double-deck bodies, four of which were front-entrance and eight were single-deck bodies fitted with 39-seat dual purpose seats and full-fronted bodywork which incorporated an AEC grille from a Regent V. All these were registered in Huddersfield as new vehicles with chassis numbers which started at 6666, the Hanson telephone number, and were built between 1956 and 1963. No 360, NCX 543, was one of the May 1960 examples.

Above:
South Yorkshire Motors Ltd based in Pontefract was the only operator to purchase lowbridge bodies with an offside gangway upstairs which were 30ft long. Mounted on a Leyland PD3/1 chassis, they were delivered in June 1960 and numbered 82 and 83. The Roe body seated 65 and was fitted with folding rear doors. No 82, 2599 WW, is seen outside the works. The only other side-gangway lowbridge bus built after this was the Liss & District AEC seen earlier on page 93.

Below:
York Pullman Bus Co Ltd, York, was a regular customer for Roe bodywork. In July 1960 an AEC Reliance was purchased with a 41-seat body fitted with dual purpose seats, luggage racks and roof windows. No 73, VDN 429, stands outside York's Castle Museum.

Above:

The building of trolleybus bodies continued after the war and it was 1965 when the last new body was supplied to Teesside RTB on a refurbished Sunbeam chassis. Typical of many rebodied chassis is Maidstone Corporation No 56, GKP 511, which was rebodied in late 1960, the chassis being a MOWT Sunbeam W4 model.

Below:

Great Yarmouth Corporation was one operator which needed 27ft- and 30ft-long double-deck buses for use on different routes. In May 1961 a convoy of new Daimler CVG6 buses prepare to leave Crossgates, numbered 109-13, FEX 109-13. The first two are 30ft long with 73 seats while the other three were 27ft-long 63-seaters.

Top and above:
After the introduction of the Roe-built Atlanteans in 1960 for the BET group, ACV built a number of bodies on 27ft-long 7ft 6in-wide chassis. The first were two batches of five for Swindon Corporation built on Daimler CVG chassis. No 118, XHR 118, one of the first batch supplied in April 1961, shows that many of the body components were based on the Atlantean design. The remaining batch was completed in July. The other

customers were the BET companies, Yorkshire Traction Co Ltd and Stratford-on-Avon Blue Motors Ltd, when six Leyland PS2 single-deck chassis 7ft 6in wide were refurbished by Yorkshire Traction and fitted with front-entrance 63-seat bodies.
Yorkshire Traction received Nos 1190-4, VHE 190-4, in July 1961, while the Stratford Blue one, No 16, JUE 353, was the only one to retain its original registration number.

Top:
When Huddersfield Corporation started abandoning its trolleybus system in 1961, the first 24 replacement vehicles were Leyland PD3/2 types with 70-seat front-entrance Roe composite bodies. At the same time Huddersfield JOC purchased six AEC Regent V buses with similar bodies; two of these are seen under construction and they were completed in January 1962.

Above:
The manager of Sunderland Corporation Transport Department, Mr Norman Morton, persuaded the council to purchase a new Daimler Fleetline with a Roe 70-seat body. No 250, SGR 250, was delivered to Sunderland in March 1962. The metal body was basically the same as the Atlantean bodies supplied to the BET companies. It was cleverly disguised by fitting peaks to the front and rear domes, and the use of a fibreglass box-type rear mudguard cover.

Above:
This photograph shows the Roe directors in late 1962. Charles Henry Roe, preparing to retire, stands in the Wulfrunian's doorway, while the other remaining directors stand in front of the bus.

Below:
In July 1961 the PSV legislation changed, allowing vehicles to be 8ft 2½in wide and up to 36ft long. The first Roe body built to take advantage of the changes was a Leyland Leopard which was fitted with a body 8ft 2½in wide, 30ft 8½in long. The 49-seat bus was for Pennine Motor Services, a small independent based at Gargrave near Skipton. It was completed in May 1963 and was registered 240 CWY.

Above:
Great Yarmouth Corporation had one-piece windscreens fitted to its three Daimler Freeline single-deck buses built in April 1964 with 43 dual-purpose seats, Nos 18-20, AEX 18-20B.

Below:
Not all customers were impressed with new ideas. Oldham Corporation purchased 10 Leyland PD3/5 double-deck buses with 73-seat composite bodies and exposed radiators once again, after having had experience of new tin fronts on previous deliveries. These were the largest buses to be used by Oldham since the withdrawal of the six-wheel double-deck buses in the early 1930s.

Top:
One of the members of the A1 service in Ayrshire, R. B. Steele, ordered a 65-seat Roe body fitted with a rear entrance and platform doors. It was completed in May 1964 on a Leyland PD2/3O chassis, 27ft long, and was registered as YCS 465.

Above
One of the orders transferred from Park Royal was the building of a 36ft by 8ft 2½in body on a Leyland Panther for the 1964 Earls Court Show in Kingston upon Hull livery. Numbered 172, BKH 172B, it was followed in 1965 by 173-8, CRH 173-8C, and then in 1966 by 179-83, GAT 179-83D. No 172 was the first 36ft body to be built at Crossgates and the dual-door, all-metal body seated 45.

Top:
Another of the 1964 Show exhibits was a Leeds City Transport Daimler Fleetline, No 101, 101 LNW. This was the first of the all-metal bodies where the appearance was improved by using a one-piece curved windscreen and the fitting of shrouds over the rear-engine compartment.

Above:
Roe built three bodies using Park Royal shells on AEC Renown chassis for Rotherham Corporation. No 88 is one of three numbered 88-90, 5588-90 ET, delivered in November 1964. Note that the upper deck is the same as the Leeds Fleetline.

Top:
Yorkshire Traction Co Ltd purchased 10 Leyland PD3A/1 buses with Roe 73-seat front-entrance bodies. This time a sliding door was fitted and the batch was numbered 1306-15, CHE 306-315C. The body is still similar to the 7ft 6in-wide ones supplied in 1961.

Above:
By late 1965, the rear-engined chassis was gaining popularity and this example for H. Wilson, Premier, was built on a Daimler Fleetline chassis. HYG 123C seated 78.

Above:
Oldham Corporation purchased a number of Leyland Atlantean double-deck buses 30ft 6in long with 77-seat Roe bodies where the appearance was improved by sloping windscreens and peaks to front and rear domes. No 143 was supplied in summer 1966.

Below:
Darlington Corporation was one operator to buy the 36ft-long Daimler Roadliner chassis. In 1967 six 48-seat dual-door examples with Roe all-metal bodies were placed into service, numbered 13-18, MHN 313-8E.

Above right:
Further improvements were made after the merger of Leyland and Daimler in 1965. This allowed the Leyland Atlantean to be fitted with a drop-centre rear axle and the 'Daimatic' gearbox from the Daimler Fleetline. This enabled the Atlantean to be offered suitable for lowbridge routes. One of the first customers was West Riding, which purchased 25 with Roe 76-seat bodies. Another customer was R. Chisnell & Sons Ltd, the owners of King Alfred Motor Services (the Winchester independent) which purchased four with identical bodies. Delivered in April 1967, they were registered HOR 589E-92E. HOR 591E is seen at Crossgates.

Above:

The last traditional Roe composite body to be built was completed in September 1968 for Northampton Corporation, numbered 267, JVV 267G, being last of a batch of five numbered 263-7. It was built on a Daimler CVG6 chassis 27ft-long and seated 59. All buses purchased by Northampton between 1947 and 1968 had been supplied with Roe bodies, with only five having metal-framed bodies. Between 1924 and 1968, 130 of the 267 buses purchased are known to have had Roe-built bodies. This is an example of customer loyalty, but it may just be a coincidence that Charles H. Roe's father was born within 20 miles of Northampton!

Above:
The Park Royal group introduced a new standard double-deck bus body in 1969. Amongst the first to be built at Crossgates were 20 dual-door 71-seat ones for Kingston upon Hull Corporation. Numbered 258-77, TKH 258-77H, they were built on Leyland Atlantean chassis and were completed in late 1969. No 266 is seen on its test run, again before delivery.

Below:
In March 1969, the Provincial Traction Co Ltd was taken over by the Wiles Group, a Hanson Trust company which specialised in asset stripping. James Hanson, one of the principals in Hanson Trust, was also Chairman of the Hanson Transport Group Ltd, which included Hanson's Buses Ltd in Huddersfield. Hanson's Buses was rumoured to have placed an order for Roe-bodied Daimler Fleetlines before it was taken over by Huddersfield Corporation in October 1969. By January 1970, when Hanson Trust sold its interests in Provincial's Gosport & Fareham Omnibus Co Ltd to the National Bus Company, Provincial had ordered for 1971 delivery six Daimler Fleetline double-deck buses with Roe bodies. Hants & Dorset Motor Services Ltd took over the administration of the company and exchanged six new Bristol RE dual-door single-deck buses for the six unwanted Daimler Fleetlines which were then delivered in June 1971 in Hants & Dorset livery, numbering 1901-6, VRU 124-9 J. No 1904 is seen prior to leaving the works.

Top:
Another customer for the dual-door body was Chesterfield Corporation, which placed eight Leyland Atlantean double-deck buses with 71-seat dual-door bodies into service in July 1972. Numbered 115-22, PNU 115-22K, the vehicles were fitted with a large side window to the rear of the upper deck instead of the usual two windows.

Above:
After fire destroyed part of the premises of East Lancashire Coachbuilders in Blackburn in 1970, SELNEC's 34 Daimler Fleetline chassis were diverted to Park Royal for the bodies to be constructed. In turn, they were passed on to Crossgates for Roe to build the Mancunian-style bodies with dual doors and 72 seats on the 33ft chassis. They were completed in early 1972, numbered 2271-304, SVR 271-304K, and were delivered to the Central division of SELNEC PTE for use in Manchester. No 2281 is seen outside the Roe works.

Above and below:
After the West Yorkshire Passenger Transport Executive was formed in 1974, both Leyland Atlantean and Daimler Fleetline chassis were purchased with similar Roe bodies seating 76 and 75 respectively. Some vehicles had a lower driving position than others. This is shown on Daimler Fleetline No 7094, WUM 94S, new in December 1977, and Leyland Atlantean No 6200, JUM 200V, new in January 1980. The last Fleetline and Atlantean were delivered in October 1978 and December 1981 respectively.

Top:
The next deliveries to WYPTE started in January 1982 when the first of 20 Leyland Olympians with Roe bodies seating 76 was completed – No 5001, UWW 1X. The last Olympian to be built at Crossgates by Roe was WYPTE No 5145, B140 RWY.

Above:
In early 1983, the Roe works were building an integral coach built on Roe-built spaceframe underframe which was fitted with Leyland mechanical parts, including the rear engine. Named the Royal Tiger Doyen, it was designed to compete with the best of the Continental coaches. No 1603, A603 KYG, was the only one to be supplied to the WYPTE MetroCoach fleet, being completed in December 1983.

Top left:
In 1967, the driver of No 64, an AEC Regent III bus owned by York Pullman Bus Co Ltd, took a wrong turning and went under a gantry which was lower than the roof of the bus. The result was a visit back to the Repair Department at Crossgates to be repaired and reroofed. Note there were no broken windows in this view on arrival at the works. Many other similar accidents were dealt with over the years, and it is a tribute to the craftsmen at Crossgates that No 64 has been owned since 1971 by Tony Peart, a Doncaster preservationist, who has taken 64 to vintage vehicle rallies all over Britain.

Left:
In 1969, one of the all-metal Daimler Fleetline buses, new in March 1968 to West Riding, was another accident victim to

have treatment at Crossgates. No 185, MHL 185F, returned to service after substantial first aid.

Above:
Another reminder of Crossgates Carriage Works is this replica Roe body designed by the author in 1983 which is shown under construction at Ribble Motor Services' Frenchwood Works, Preston in 1984. It was completed in early 1985, and painted in Ribble colours rather than the intended York Corporation livery when the project began. The chassis is a Leyland Lion PLSC3, VY 957. The original body on VY 957 was built in May 1929 and was supplied to York Corporation with fleet No 2. In 1998 the present owner of this restored vehicle, Stagecoach, has placed it on loan for display at the Greater Manchester Museum of Transport.

9. Optare, 1984 to date

Following the closure of the C. H. Roe factory by Leyland in 1984, a group of former senior managers decided to pool their knowledge and expertise and restart operations using their redundancy payments. They initially operated from an office in Bradford (c/o Davenport Engineering, 72 Harris Street) for a month from 5 November 1984, moving back to Crossgates for the new year, and used the 'off-the-shelf' name 'Simco No 49 Ltd', with registered offices at 41 Park Square, Leeds.

Mr Russell Richardson, a former plant director, by this time in a similar position with Duple, was invited to become Managing Director. A competition was held within the small band of original shareholders for a name for the company in time for reoccupation of the Carriage Works. Optare, Latin for 'to choose' was to be the name for what was to become a leader in style and innovation.

Negotiations between British Leyland, the West Yorkshire Enterprise Board and Mr Richardson resulted in Leyland selling the premises to the Board, which in turn leased them over 20 years to Optare. The factory opened for business on 15 February 1985, recruiting former employees for whom purchase of shares was a condition of employment. Originally, only the offices and finishing shops were occupied by Optare, the rest of the buildings being acquired as the company grew.

The first order was from South Yorkshire PTE for Dennis Domino 33-seat midibuses, the first vehicle of which was completed only 15 weeks after the reopening of the works. Among the early orders was a batch of ambulances based on Renault Master vans for Durham Ambulance Services, and a batch of Freight Rover Sherpa minibuses supplied to West Yorkshire PTE in 1985 hinted at future innovations. Despite being 16-seat van conversions, they incorporated several 'big bus' features, including full-height, four-leaf jack-knife doors, and a full-height centre rear emergency exit. Fifteen Olympians and 15 Domino-style bodies on Leyland Cub chassis completed the West Yorkshire PTE order. Later, the Olympian part of the order was reduced to 10 vehicles: three as standard buses, five as coach-seated express buses and two as convertible open-toppers which were used on normal services in Leeds!

The Leyland Cubs were delivered in the winter of 1986, 11 being 35-seat stage carriage buses whilst the balance had 33 dual-purpose seats and optimistically sported 'MetroCoach' fleetnames. The marriage of the neat Domino-style body (by now known as the Nipper) with the Cub chassis was not a happy one, as the

Leyland Terrier box van chassis from which the Cub was derived was just not up to the job. Most found new ownership before their first anniversary!

The five apparently cancelled Olympians turned out to be merely postponed, appearing in spring 1986, fitted with coach seats and lively TL11 engines. Leeds City Council production continued with the production of Dodge welfare vehicles, and two full-sized mobile libraries on Ford R series chassis, complete with Olympian fronts.

The new era of deregulation was looming, and Optare was gearing up to supply the needs of the new-style operator. The revolutionary CityPacer 25 made its debut in late spring 1986, setting the pace of future production in many ways, not least in its futuristic styling. It was built on a heavier variant of the VW LT chassis not normally available in Britain, the LT 55. Considerable changes were made to the chassis, including a shift of driving position, both up and rear-ward. The high driving position not only ensured superb driver visibility, but also a commanding view of the entrance and steps. The first five for London Buses subsidiary, Orpington Buses, were followed by a further 44 for use in central London. During the period when these 25-seat buses were built, all other minibuses were 16-20-seat van conversions. As the industry was getting used to a slightly larger small bus, Optare produced another surprise. The 33-seat Mercedes Benz 811D-based StarRider appeared in the summer of 1987 and though it used a similar structure to the CityPacer, it featured slightly less radical styling. The chassis was extended, both within the wheelbase and again in the rear overhang, having an overall length of 8.4m. Other builders followed this lead, and, ultimately, Mercedes-Benz offered a chassis of this length. These small buses set the scene for the future, both being based on unique exclusive partnerships and each producing a complete product for which Optare held after-sales responsibility.

This sort of arrangement had been seen before. During Mr Richardson's time at Duple, he had been responsible for the production of 100 Bova Calypso coaches, a unique combination of Caribbean-style Duple coach bodies and Bova underframe. Further double-deck deliveries on Olympian chassis were for Maidstone Borough Council, Cambus, and some dual-door examples for Reading Transport. Ironically, a further batch for Reading, this time coach-seated express versions, was subcontracted from Leyland as it was experiencing production difficulties at its Workington plant.

Sales of the StarRider continued apace, with large orders going to London Buses. Incorporating the 'fast-flow' full-size doorway, others were for Badgerline and many individual ones were built as coaches. At the time it was a bestseller and, apart from the large orders mentioned, sales were often made up of threes, twos and many individual vehicles.

In October 1988, the CityPacer was redesignated, being marketed with options grouped in packages. This month also saw the launch of the Delta at the NEC Motor Show.

This time the exclusive partnership was three-way, combining the style for which Optare had become renowned, the smoothness of the DAF SB220 chassis and the revolutionary but well proven Alusuisse 'sticky bolt' and extrusion construction. Marketed as Britain's smoothest, quietest bus, there was at the time little to compete with it.

1988 was an eventful year: as well as the developments documented above, Mr Russell Richardson was awarded the MBE. In July 1989, Optare acquired the 'assets, rights, and intellectual properties' of MCW, bringing with it the designs and jigs for Metrorider production. The Metrobus was included in the deal, later being transformed beyond recognition into the Spectra, together with the single- and double-deck Metroliner (both of which were shelved). Though the Metrorider was sound in design, construction and finish left a lot to be desired. Options on the driveline were reduced, leaving the most popular option, the naturally aspirated Cummins 6B and Allison AT545 automatic transmission, as the only choice. Operator-friendly changes included the substitution of steel side panels by conventional aluminium panelling and glass-fibre skirt panels, and gasket glazing replaced bonding for ease of repair. The first 'Optare-ised' MetroRider appeared at Coach and Bus '89: Ipswich Buses' No 221, looking very 'municipal' with its large fleetnames and coats of arms. From then on, the Metroliner adopted Optare-lettering of a single word with a second capital letter ie MetroRider.

The next announcement was for the launch of the MAN-based 'Vecta' in February 1991. Often seen as a competitive response to the Dennis Dart, it actually came first, but sales were initially slow. Based on the MAN 11.190, another exclusive chassis, it effectively used a shortened form of the Alusuisse Delta body, and was 10m long by a full 2.5m wide.

In the autumn of 1990, a merger was announced with the United Bus Group. Founder members DAF Bus and BOVA had formed United Bus, and Optare became the third partner, soon followed by DAB of Denmark, Den Oudsten and, finally, Ramseier & Jenzer of Switzerland. The group ranked sixth in size in the West European bus market with a turnover of £184 million. The aim of the partnership was to create economies of scale by pooling resources in research and development. It did, indeed, seem to be the ideal partnership for all concerned giving as it did autonomy with regard to individual companies' policies with the backup of a large group.

Autumn 1991 brought the launch of the Spectra, a new double-deck bus designed jointly with fellow United Bus member, DAF Bus, and which used Alusuisse body technology to even more striking effect. A low-emission 'quiet' 260bhp DAF engine, as well as common componentry with the Delta, produced a very sophisticated double-deck bus. The first Spectra entered service with Reading Buses in March 1992, followed by 24 for London Central, one dual-door example for Metroline, and one for East Yorkshire Motor Services. Later deliveries were to Reading Buses, Stevenson's, Istanbul and Izmir, Turkey, and the first of a large fleet for Wilts & Dorset.

October 1993, unfortunately, witnessed the collapse of the United Bus Group, following the failure of Den Oudsten owing to the state of its domestic market. During subsequent months each of the group members passed back into independent ownership.

The independent company's launch, which again featured employee shareholding, was quickly followed by the appearance of another new product. Called the 'Sigma', it combined the Vecta front with the full-length structure of the Delta, though Finite Analysis Testing required respaced pillars for maximum rigidity on the Dennis Lance chassis. Early orders came from Ipswich Buses, Trent, Go-Ahead Gateshead and Go-Ahead subsidiary, Brighton & Hove.

Further expansion of the range came with the launch of the Mercedes-Benz O.405-based Prisma, which gained popularity with operators large and small. GRT took batches of double-glazed air-conditioned examples, and at the other end of the scale, Skye-Ways bought one and MacEwan of Amisfield bought two for the high profile Borders Rail Link service.

Body numbers were originally sequential, irrespective of vehicle type, being 'J' for 'Job' followed by the number, up to J759 (the last StarRider order for London Buses). A new system, grouping types together, began with J1000 – a Kentish Bus MetroRider delivered in October 1989.

The MetroRider was always Optare's bestseller, being in service with fleets large and small all over the country. London's was easily the largest, but since that fleet has become fragmented that distinction now goes to Wilts & Dorset.

Having established itself as a manufacturer of integral buses with the MetroRider, the Excel, a rear-engined, low-floor integral bus, was announced at the 1994 NEC Show. It is available in four wheelbase lengths, giving overall lengths from 9.6m to 11.5m, and capacities from 36 to 48; the front and rear ends of the structure are common to all models, and the section between the axles determines the overall length. A major engineering advantage of the bus is the quick-change engine, made possible by the use of self-sealing fluid pipes. Deliveries so far include East Yorkshire, Trent, Cardiff, Harris Bus, Happy Al's and the Travel West Midlands 'subsidiary' Travel London.

The latest product follows a similar theme. It, too, is a low-floor integral design, fitted with a four-cylinder rear-mounted Mercedes-Benz engine, resulting in the lowest floor of any midibus. So low, in fact, as to make the Solo unique! Optare stalwart Wilts & Dorset by early 1998 had ordered 85 Solos, the first 31 of which had started work by the summer. The company, originally through United Bus membership, has also been responsible for sales of Bova coaches, but since the acquisition of Autobus of Rotherham brought about a restructuring of the company, sales of both ranges are handled by group subsidiary, CoachSales.

A notable feature is the development of export markets, starting with the delivery of two StarRiders to Luxembourg in 1988, MetroRiders to Norway in 1992, and Spectras to the Turkish cities of Istanbul and Izmir in 1994.

Exports turned into Technology Transfer arrangements, the first of which involved the Malaysian Government and local bus, truck and car manufacturer DRB building 1,000 31-seat MetroRiders at a specially built factory. The vehicles, renamed 'PekanRider' (PeopleRider), feature air-conditioning and tinted glazing and are assembled using a kit of parts shipped from the Leeds factory. In addition, a joint venture company, Optare Malta was formed with two local companies in Malta – Alpine Holdings, a Maltese importer, and the Zammit Group, a General Motors dealership – to supply a Maltese version of the Excel. Another joint venture, with the Itochu Group of Japan and Ceylinco of Sri Lanka, named Ceymo Automobile, builds the ColomboRider, a dual-door 10m-long bus based upon the Chinese Chaoyong diesel chassis. The latest agreement was announced towards the end of 1997, in which the Austral Pacific Group is to import the MetroRider in chassis form for sale in Australia and New Zealand with locally built bodywork.

Left:
South Yorkshire PTE Dennis Domino SD1202/126 No 54, C54 HDT, new in August 1985, is seen on loan to Yorkshire Rider in 1987.
Tony Greaves

Below left:
Seen descending towards Lowerhouses near Huddersfield is Leyland Cub C810 KBT, originally West Yorkshire PTE No 1810. Acquired from Cedarbus, Worthing by K Line, it still carries signwritten advertising for a Worthing estate agent. Many would feel that it was more suited to Worthing terrain.
Geoff Lumb

Above:
Seen when new on display in Bradford's Interchange is West Yorkshire PTE No 5511, C511 KBT, a Leyland TL11-engined Olympian, which was the only one of the type to carry this four-tone blue and white 'White Rose Express' livery. *WYPTE*

Right:
Seen on Brompton Road is London Buses VW CityPacer on service C1, marketed at the time as 'The Smart Little Bus around town'. They were often to be seen loaded to capacity.
Tony Greaves courtesy Optare

Above
Blackpool CityPacer No 582, the last of a fleet of 35 of the type, commemorates a charity run from Paris. *Tony Greaves*

Below:
London's second Delta was delivered to London General and used experimentally on the Red Arrow routes. Caution prevailed, however, and the Red Arrows were to remain the preserve of short Nationals. *Tony Greaves*

Above:
Harrow Buses StarRider No SR89, G89 KUB, shows off its 'Fastflow' door on route H12. *Tony Greaves, courtesy Optare*

Below:
A pair of Deltas for the new Crosville Wales company were delivered in March 1989. Both featured the 'Bws Gwynedd' red front, signifying the county council's financial support for their intended routes. *Tony Greaves, courtesy Optare*

Above:
The C1 route's growth led to the replacement of the CityPacers by long MetroRiders. London General No MRL195, J695 CGK, is seen before the application of 'Streetline' identity. *Tony Greaves, courtesy Optare*

Below:
A PMT Delta is seen when new as a member of 'The Potteries Connection', prior to the encroachment of Badgers. *Tony Greaves*

122

Above:
N204 NHS was one of a batch of MetroRiders delivered to Clydeside during early 1996. They have since been joined by six 23-seaters from West Riding.
Tony Greaves, courtesy Optare

Below:
Half of the 1994 Black Prince batch of Vectas demonstrates that operator's penchant for individual livery application.
Tony Greaves, courtesy Optare

Above:
The following year Black Prince received a Prisma, based on a Mercedes-Benz O.405 underframe, which was built between large batches of similar buses for the GRT group.
Tony Greaves, courtesy Optare

Below:
SMT Lothians Prisma N65 CSC seen on service to Bathgate.
Tony Greaves

Above:
East Yorkshire No 275, P275 NRH, a 10.7m-long version of the integral low-floor Excel loads in Hull, bound for Hessle.
Tony Greaves

Below:
Reading Buses P913 GJM dedicated to 'Fast Track' park and ride services is followed by another example in fleet livery.
Tony Greaves